The Experts Handbook
Of
Exorcism

How to Cast Out Devils

Dr. Michael H Yeager

Copyright © 2016 Dr Michael H Yeager
All rights reserved.
ISBN: 1533115648
ISBN-13:9781533115645

DEDICATION

We dedicate this book to those who are truly hungry and thirsty to live in the realm of the super natural, and to those who have already tasted of the heavenly realm. We dedicate this to the bride of Christ, those who are called to go deeper, higher, and farther than they have yet experienced. It is only by the grace that comes by FAITH in CHRIST that we will be able to accomplish His will on this earth

Introduction

Casting out devils is not something that should ever be taken lightly. We are living in a day and age were more and more people are needing to be delivered from demonic powers. Doc yeager has over 40 years of experience when it comes to casting out devils and helping people to be delivered from demonic afflictions. His first experience with a demon possessed person was in 1975. He had only been a Christian for about a month. In that particular situation, he was dealing with a devil worshiper from California who was completely demonized. The man was gloriously delivered.

This book is filled with many experiences from the author and others. In this book, you will discover important steps and Spiritual truths that will help the reader set others free. Plus you will discover how demons can take possession of people, and how people when they are delivered what they must do to stay free!

GOD Said: You Better Not Lie or You'll Die!

One day I picked up a book by a well-known author. This book had come highly recommended by one of my favorite preachers at that time. The topic was about angelic visitations. This was something I was interested in, because of my many experiences with the supernatural. I began to read this book and noticed immediately that there were experiences he said he had which did not seem to line up with the Scriptures. I did not want to judge his heart, but we do have the responsibility to examine everything in light of God's Word. If it does not line up with the word of God, then we must reject it, no matter who wrote it.

As I was pondering the stories in this book, the Spirit of the Lord spoke to my heart very strongly. It was as if He was standing right there next to me, speaking audibly. What He spoke to me was rather shocking! The Lord told me that the writer of this book would be dead in three months from a heart attack. I asked the Lord why He was telling me this. He said the stories in the man's book were exaggerated, and judgment was coming. The Lord warned me that day that if I were ever to do the same thing, judgment would come to me. I did not realize that the Lord would have me to be writing books, many them filled with my own personal experiences. Now I know why he spoke this to me, telling me that I better not exaggerate my experiences.

When the Spirit of the Lord spoke this to me, I turned and told my wife. I held the book up and said, in a very quiet whispering, trembling, wavering voice, "Honey, the man who wrote this book will be dead in three months from a heart attack." Plus, I told her why the Lord told me this. I wish I had been wrong. Exactly 3 months later, the man died from a heart attack. God can speak to us through the positive and the negative circumstances of life. We better take heed to what he is saying.

The Experts Handbook of Exorcism

CONTENTS

ACKNOWLEDGMENTS

*To our heavenly Father and His wonderful love.

*To our Lord, Savior and Master — Jesus Christ, Who saved us and set us free because of His great love for us.

*To the Holy Spirit, Who leads and guides us into the realm of truth and miraculous living every day.

*To all of those who had a part in helping me get this book ready for the publishers.

*To my Lovely Wife, and our precious children, Michael, Daniel, Steven, Stephanie, Catherine Yu, who is our precious daughter-in-law, and Naomi, who is now with the Lord.

Important Introduction

The **DELIVERANCES** I have seen, experienced, and share in this book are all true. They have happened personally to me, my family and others. These events are recalled and shared to the best of my ability.

The Authors Stories are Marked With A *

By no means do the following stories account for all the healings and miracles that we have seen, and experienced in my live. If we would recount every single answer to prayer, and every wonderful healing, miracle, and blessing, there would be no end to this book!

What I am about to share with you in this book are simply some highlights of what we have experienced in the Lord. Some of these experiences will seem to be incredulous. However, they are true. This is not a testimony of how spiritual we are, but how wonderful and marvelous the Father, the Son, and the Holy Ghost are! I share these experiences to the best of my recollections and understanding. Not every conversation I share in these experiences are exactly word for word. I would love to name every person that was a part of these wonderful occurrences, but privacy laws do not allow this. If you are reading this book and you saw, experienced, or were a part of these events, please do not be offended because your names were not mentioned.

CHAPTER ONE

*1. Devil Worshiper Delivered By the Power of God!

My first encounter with a demon possessed man was in 1975. I had only been a Christian for about two months, and I was in the Navy at the time. I was stationed on a military base on Adak, Alaska. One night (at about 8 pm) I was witnessing in my dormitory room to three men doing a bible study with them. While sharing biblical truths with these three men, another man entered my room. We called him TJ. This individual had always been very different and strange. He was kind of out there. I had never even spoken to him up to that time, except one night when he showed a nasty movie to the guys in his dorm. I had walked out of his room not being able to handle his level of filth!

When TJ entered my room, he took over my bible study and began to preach some weird off-the-wall things about the devil. He said he was from California where he had been part of a satanic church. He showed us the ends of his fingers in which some of the ends were missing from the first joint out. He told us that he had eaten them for power, and he had drunk human blood at satanic worship services. As he spoke, there seemed to be an invisible power speaking through him. An evil and demonic darkness descended upon us in my dormitory. A visible demonic power took him over right in front of our eyes, with his eyes filled with a malevolent glow! One of the guys who were in my room,

1

Hussein (who was a Muslim) declared this was too much for him, and left the room. The other two, Bobby and Willie, sat and listened.

I had never encountered anything as sinister and evil as this ever before. I honestly didn't know what to do at that time, so I went downstairs to the barracks right below me. There was a fellow Christian I had the opportunity of working with who lived right below me. After I had given my heart to Jesus Christ, Willie, the cowboy told me that he too was a born again, Spirit-filled Christian. I had yet to see the evidence of this in Willie's life, but I didn't know where else to go. I went down to his room and knocked on Willie's door. When he opened the door, I explained to him what was happening in my room. I was able to get him to come to my room upstairs. Willie stepped into my dormitory and stopped. We both saw that TJ was now up on a stool that was made from a log, and he preaching under the power of satanic spirits. At that very moment cowboy Willie turned tail and ran out of my room. I went after him. He told me that he had no idea what to do and that he could not handle this. He left me standing outside by my door alone.

I went back into my room and did the only thing I could, I cried out to Jesus Christ. The minute I cried out looking up towards heaven, I'm telling you that a bright light from heaven shone right through my ceiling. It was a beam of light that was about 3 feet wide, an all glistening bright light, shining upon me. I do not know if anyone else in my room saw this bright light. All I know is the Spirit of God rose up within me, and I was overwhelmed with God's presence.

My mouth was instantly filled with an amazingly powerful and prophetic word from heaven. I began to preach **Jesus Christ** by the power of the spirit! As I began to speak by the spirit, the power of God fell in that room. The next thing I knew was that TJ had dropped to the floor like a rock. TJ began to squirming just like a snake his body bending and twisting in I an impossible way. There was no fear left in my heart as I watched this demonic activity. There was nothing but a Holy Ghost boldness and divine inspiration flowing through me at that time.

Now during this divine encounter of Heaven both Willie and Bobby had fallen on their knees crying out to Jesus to save them. At the same time they gave their hearts to the Lord, and they were both instantly filled with the Holy Ghost! The next thing I knew I found myself kneeling over the top of TJ as he was squirming like a snake. I placed my hands upon him. Willie and Bobby came over at the same time joining me and laid their hands upon TJ also. With a voice of authority inspired by the Spirit, I commanded the demons to come out of the man in the Name of Jesus Christ. As God is my witness, we all heard three to five different voices come screaming out of TJ! After the demons were gone it was like TJ breathed a last long breath like that of a dying man, and grew completely still. After a while, he opened up his eyes that were now filled with complete peace. At that very moment, he gave his heart to Jesus Christ. I led him into the baptism of the Holy Ghost. The presence of God overwhelmed all of us as we gave praise and thanks to the Lord. The next Sunday these three men went with me to church.

Evil Personified

TJ, the man who I had cast the demons cast out of, came to my room one night. His heart was filled with great fear because he had been so deeply involved in the satanic realm. He was hearing satanic voices telling him that they were going to kill him. One night as I was sleeping, TJ began to scream. He was yelling that the devil was there to kill him! I sat up in my bunk and looked around. From the position of my bed, I saw the light of the moon shining through our big plate glass window. There on our wall was a shadow of a larger demonic entity. I was not making this up.

This entity moved across the room toward TJ. The very atmosphere of the room was filled with a terrible presence of evil. Fear tried to rise within my heart, but the Spirit of God quickened courage and boldness within me. I rose up out of my bed, commanded this demonic power to leave our room and never return in the name of Jesus Christ of Nazareth. The minute I spoke to it in the name of Jesus, I heard a screeching voice like finger nails scraping across a chalk board. The shadow began to be pulled out of the room as if a gigantic vacuum cleaner had been turned on, and it was being sucked up by an invisible force. This demonic power never came back again.

This Is WAR!

We Must Not Be Ignorant of the Devils Devices!

*Revelation 12:7 And there was war in heaven: Michael and his angels fought against the dragon; and the dragon fought and his angels,

There is a war that is raging all around us. It began in the book of Genesis, and we see its completion in the very last chapter of the book of Revelation. The word **war** is used 220 times in the Bible, **battle** 171 times, **fight** 103 times, **Army** 73 times. This is a supernatural warfare, a conflict, a battle with to opposing sides. As a human being you are either in the fight with God against the powers of darkness, or you have been made a captive, a prisoner, a victim of demonic forces.

2 Timothy 2:25 In meekness instructing those that oppose themselves; if God peradventure will give them repentance to the acknowledging of the truth;26 And that they may recover themselves out of the snare of the devil, who are taken captive by him at his will.

Ephesians 6:12 - For we wrestle not against flesh and blood, but against principalities, against powers, against the rulers of the darkness of this world, against spiritual wickedness in high [places].

I2 Corinthians 10:3-5 - For though we walk in the flesh, we do not war after the flesh:

Ephesians 6:13 - Wherefore take unto you the whole armour of God, that ye may be able to withstand in the evil day, and having done all, to stand.

Deuteronomy 28:7 - The LORD shall cause thine enemies that rise up against thee to be smitten before thy face: they shall come out against thee one way, and flee before thee seven ways.

---

2 Corinthians 10:4 (For the weapons of our warfare are not carnal, but mighty through God to the pulling down of strong holds;)

---

1 Timothy 1:18 This charge I commit unto thee, son Timothy, according to the prophecies which went before on thee, that thou by them mightest war a good warfare;

---

2 Timothy 2:4 No man that warreth entangleth himself with the affairs of this life; that he may please him who hath chosen him to be a soldier.

---

*1 Peter 2:11 Dearly beloved, I beseech you as strangers and pilgrims, abstain from fleshly lusts, which war against the soul;

---

*Revelation 17:14 These shall make war with the Lamb, and the Lamb shall overcome them: for he is Lord of lords, and King of kings: and they that are with him are called, and chosen, and faithful.

Ignorance Will Kill You!

Being sincere will not help you in the midst of the battle. Taking on demonic powers is one of the most serious and deadly things you can do. Untold numbers have been destroyed because they had no knowledge, or incorrect knowledge when dealing with these invisible but very real entities. You might say that they were shooting into the dark. Completely oblivious and blind to the fact of what was going on in the spiritual realm. That's why Jesus proclaimed boldly: **you shall know the truth, and the truth will make you free.**

Let me first say that if you are not born again, spirit filled, and passionate about Jesus Christ you better not be trying to cast out devils and demons that are tormenting people. There is an example of seven brothers who were the sons of a priest who endeavored to do this. The results were devastating.

Acts 19:11 And God wrought special miracles by the hands of

Paul:12 So that from his body were brought unto the sick handkerchiefs or aprons, and the diseases departed from them, and the evil spirits went out of them.13 Then certain of the vagabond Jews, exorcists, took upon them to call over them which had evil spirits the name of the Lord Jesus, saying, We adjure you by Jesus whom Paul preacheth.14 And there were seven sons of one Sceva, a Jew, and chief of the priests, which did so.15 And the evil spirit answered and said, Jesus I know, and Paul I know; but who are ye?16 And the man in whom the evil spirit was leaped on them, and overcame them, and prevailed against them, so that they fled out of that house naked and wounded.

Even many of those who proclaim to know Christ are completely ignorant and blind to how God works. A good example of this is when Eve was being tempted of the devil. Why did God not come to her help? Here is the simple answer: she did not cry out, and ask for his help! If she would have simply cried out to God, and asked for his help, he would have been there faster than you could snap your fingers. Many have accused God of horrendous crimes because they did not know their **adversary**, and did not understand who **God** is, or how he works.

*Hosea 4:6 My people are destroyed for lack of knowledge: because thou hast rejected knowledge, I will also reject thee, that thou shalt be no priest to me: seeing thou hast forgotten the law of thy God, I will also forget thy children.

*Isaiah 5:13 Therefore my people are gone into captivity, because they have no knowledge: and their honourable men are famished, and their multitude dried up with thirst.

*2 Corinthians 4:3 But if our gospel be hid, it is hid to them that

are lost:4 In whom the god of this world hath blinded the minds of them which believe not, (the word of God) lest the light of the glorious gospel of Christ, who is the image of God, should shine unto them.5 For we preach not ourselves, but Christ Jesus the Lord; and ourselves your servants for Jesus' sake.

*Hosea 4:4 Hear the word of the Lord, ye children of Israel: for the Lord hath a controversy with the inhabitants of the land, because there is no truth, nor mercy, nor knowledge of God in the land.

*2 Peter 3:5 For this they willingly are ignorant of, that by the word of God the heavens were of old, and the earth standing out of the water and in the water:

*James 1:13 Let no man say when he is tempted, I am tempted of God: for God cannot be tempted with evil, neither tempteth he any man:

*James 4:2 Ye lust, and have not: ye kill, and desire to have, and cannot obtain: ye fight and war, yet ye have not, because ye ask not.

*Job 42:2 I know that thou canst do everything, and that no thought can be withholden from thee.3 Who is he that hideth counsel without knowledge? therefore have I uttered that I understood not; things too wonderful for me, which I knew not...........5 I have heard of thee by the hearing of the ear: but now mine eye seeth thee.6 Wherefore I abhor myself, and repent in dust and ashes.

2 Corinthians 11:3 But I fear, lest by any means, as the serpent beguiled Eve through his subtilty, so your minds should be corrupted from the simplicity that is in Christ.

2 Corinthians 2:11 Lest Satan should get an advantage of us: for we are not ignorant of his devices.

Understanding Your Enemy

The satanic world is composed of demonic spirits who were formerly angels and disembodied creatures who followed Lucifer in his rebellious treason against God. The very fiber of their moral character has been totally perverted and demoralized. There remains not even a sliver or spark of repentance. There is no love, mercy, sympathy, or kindness in their bosoms. They are murderers, liars, blasphemers, haters of mankind, propagators of the most horrible and outrageous crimes against creation, against man and God.

Many of the fallen angels appear to men like angels of light, so-called "guardians of mystical secrets." They sell their wares to gullible, money-seeking, self-gratifying, power-hungry humans. They appear in many forms promising immortality and limitless authority. They tote lies as the truth, declaring new revelations and higher realms of enlightenment. They push karma and New-Age theologies that deceive men and who have in turn deceived others. Even as the father of lies appeared to Adam and his wife in the Garden of Eden, so they follow the same pattern, promising that which they cannot give because they do not possess it. By their deceptions and perversions, they capture their prey as a spider captures a fly in its web, spinning a cocoon of lies around about their minds and emotions and slowly but surely injecting the deadly venom to possess and devour them. Much of their deceptions are woven with biblical truths and principles taken out of context.

They teach a Christianity that uses God, instead of one that surrenders its will and life to God. In the garden, Satan told Eve that she could eat of the Tree of the Knowledge of good and evil and not die. In the same way, the lie is still being propagated today to the masses of gullible people that we can continue to partake of good and evil and still live and not die. It is a lie that we can be like God and keep living in willful rebellion and disobedience. But true Christianity that brings salvation seeks the perfect will of God and reflects a life that hungers and thirsts after true holiness and righteousness.

These fallen angelic beings have only one purpose of existence, and that is to **POSSESS, CONTROLE,** and to totally destroy anyone or anything that resembles the splendid nature of the glory of the Creator. They have fallen from their original glory and will never be able to ascend again to that magnificent position. For there is no repentance, nor forgiveness, nor redemption for these pitiful, lowly, corrupted beings that are destined to everlasting torment and damnation in the lake of fire, where the fire is never quenched, and the worm never dies.

Many have given heed to their seductive and damnable heresies, refusing to obey God and to turn from their wicked ways. Instead, they reach and strive for that forbidden fruit that even Lucifer grasped for in order to become God, which is the impossible, unattainable, and corrupted dream. For that which is created can never become greater or equal to the One who created him. It is like a gnat endeavoring to become an Eagle or the clay pot longing to become the Potter. Even as Lucifer lusted after God's power, position, anointing, and authority, many today who have been deceived into believing that they are Christians are hungering and lusting after the same things. In truth, they should be longing for nothing but to be **just like Jesus in his character and nature**. Through Christ, God has given His sons and daughters the privilege to rule and reign with Him forever.

*John 8:44 Ye are of your father the devil, and the lusts of your father ye will do. He was a murderer from the beginning, and abode not in the truth because there is no truth in him. When he speaketh a lie, he speaketh of his own: for he is a liar and the father of it.

*John 10:10 The thief cometh not, but for to steal, and to kill, and to destroy: I am come that they might have life, and that they might have it more abundantly.

*Job 1:7 And the Lord said unto Satan, Whence comest thou? Then Satan answered the Lord, and said, From going to and fro in the earth, and from walking up and down in it.

*Job 2:7 So went Satan forth from the presence of the Lord, and smote Job with sore boils from the sole of his foot unto his crown.

*Acts 10:38 How God anointed Jesus of Nazareth with the Holy Ghost and with power: who went about doing good, and healing all that were oppressed of the devil; for God was with him.

*Psalm 106:37 Yea, they sacrificed their sons and their daughters unto devils,

*Ephesians 4:27 Neither give place to the devil.

Ephesians 6:11 Put on the whole armour of God, that ye may be able to stand against the wiles of the devil.

1 Timothy 4:1 Now the Spirit speaketh expressly, that in the latter times some shall depart from the faith, giving heed to seducing spirits, and doctrines of devils;

2 Timothy 2:26 And that they may recover themselves out of the snare of the devil, who are taken captive by him at his will.

Hebrews 2:14 Forasmuch then as the children are partakers of flesh and blood, he also himself likewise took part of the same; that through death he might destroy him that had the power of death, that is, the devil;

James 2:19 Thou believest that there is one God; thou doest well: the devils also believe, and tremble.

James 3:15 This wisdom descendeth not from above, but is earthly, sensual, devilish.16 For where envying and strife is, there is confusion and every evil work.

James 4:7 Submit yourselves therefore to God. Resist the devil, and he will flee from you.

1 Peter 5:8 Be sober, be vigilant; because your adversary the devil, as a roaring lion, walketh about, seeking whom he may devour:

1 John 3:8 He that committeth sin is of the devil; for the devil

sinneth from the beginning. For this purpose the Son of God was manifested, that he might destroy the works of the devil.

---

*Revelation 12:9 And the great dragon was cast out, that old serpent, called the Devil, and Satan, which deceiveth the whole world: he was cast out into the earth, and his angels were cast out with him.

---

*Revelation 20:10 And the devil that deceived them was cast into the lake of fire and brimstone, where the beast and the false prophet are, and shall be tormented day and night for ever and ever

Don't Be Surprised When the Enemy Attacks

In the last 40 years whenever I have had to deal with demonic powers there has always been repercussions. What I mean by this is that when you deal with the enemy, he is going to respond by attacking you. I'm not saying this to create within you any fear of what he can do. **I'm simply stating a fact that is true.** You just have to be prepared by having your heart filled with the word of God and faith to respond to these attacks. Let me share one of these examples with you.

*2. Demonic power tried to kill me! (1977)

Here I was as a 21-year-old kid on-fire for God! I knew in my heart I was stirring things up in the satanic realm and the demonic world would try to find a way to destroy me. I did not have any fear in my heart because I had discovered the truth that *"greater is He that is in me, than he that is in the world!"*

Now I had a very realistic experience one night as I was sleeping. I saw this dark, faceless demon come running down the long hallway of the house I was staying in. It was just a tiny house that had been a chicken house converted into a small house with a guest quarters. I shared this house with an evangelist and his wife. I slept all the way down on the other side of this long narrow building. I'm not complaining (faith never grumbles or gripes). I could handle it even if it was not heated or air conditioned. The particular night, I saw in a very tangible dream this demonic spirit come running down this long hallway through the door and into my bedroom. When it came into my bedroom, it immediately jumped on top of me and began choking me. I could not physically breathe at that moment. Panic and fear overwhelmed me! Then I heard the voice of God speak to my heart, telling me to be at peace.

The Lord's presence came flooding in upon me at that very moment. I cried out to Jesus with a whisper and rebuked this demon that was choking me, in the name of Jesus. At this point, I was fully awake by this time. As this dark image continued choking me, I saw a gigantic hand come down through the ceiling of my room. It grabbed this faceless, dark demonic power around the neck and ripped it off me. This gigantic hand shook it like a cat would a mouse and threw it out of the room. God's presence overwhelmed me as I was sitting up in my bed crying and weeping with joy and praising God! This experience was not just my imagination running wild, but it was literal and real!

CHAPTER TWO

Christ Has Given Us Power Over Demonic Forces!

Then the seventy returned with joy, saying, "Lord, even the demons are subject to us in Your name."
And He said to them, "I saw Satan fall like lightning from heaven.

"Behold, I give you the authority to trample on serpents and scorpions, and over all the power of the enemy, and nothing shall by any means hurt you.

"Nevertheless do not rejoice in this, that the spirits are subject to you, but rather rejoice because your names are written in heaven" (Luke 10:17-20 NKJV).

The Following is Written **by: Rick Joyner**

Christians have been given authority over demons, yet very few even understand it, much less use it. There are even sincere Christians who believe that demons or the devil do not exist, but are metaphors for serious human problems. Though one does not have to believe in the devil to be saved, such beliefs which are in direct conflict with the Scriptures have to be one of the devil's most effective deceptions. The devil dwells in darkness or hiddenness. If he can make Christians believe that he does not exist, he has certainly been successful at hiding himself.

Other Christians believe that demons existed in biblical times, but think that they just disappeared somehow after the first century. Others think they are still here, but are all in Africa or the South American jungles. Still, others think that they are not only still here, but have been having babies and multiplying since the first century! These tend to see demons behind everything. What is the truth about this, and how can knowing the truth affect our lives?

As is often the case, the truth is found between the extremes. Demonic forces are a much bigger problem than many suppose, and the ignorance of those who do not know how they operate or the authority we have been given over them, are far more vulnerable to the schemes of the devil. Of course, there are some who go too far, believing that the devil or demons are the cause of every human problem. It is going to be increasingly important for us to understand this issue and walk in the authority we have been given over the powers of evil.

Our Authority

True spiritual authority comes from abiding in the King. We have authority **"in His name,"** which implies that we have His authority when we are on a mission for Him. There is a general assignment that we all have as Christians, which gives us general authority in that area. There are also specific assignments that we are given individually or as groups which give us more specific authority in areas. There is a reason why the Lord told His followers that He was sending them out to heal the sick and cast out devils. When you are sent out by Him to do His work, you will stir up the evil one, and you will need to deal with him.

Even though we would do well to spend much more time seeking to understand the Lord and His ways than the devil and his ways, we are commanded not to be ignorant of the devil's schemes. Those who are ignorant of them are going to be paying an increasingly high price for that ignorance. We must know and learn to use the authority that we have over the powers of evil.

The discerning knows that we have as serious a demonic problem in the West as anywhere else in the world. Some forms of civilization enable demonic forces to be more easily disguised. Some demonic forces are simply more socially acceptable, but the good side of the Tree of Knowledge is just as deadly as the evil side. In relation to demonic powers, this means that seemingly "nice" demons, or to use the biblical term, "angels of light" (see II Corinthians 11:14) that are in fact fallen angels, are just as evil, and result in just as much bondage and death.

When an angel of light is de-masked, it will show itself as hideously evil and cruel as any released by the witchcraft practiced by even the most uncivilized tribes in the Southern hemispheres. This is what the world found out through Nazi Germany, one of the most cultured and civilized nations in the world when it fell under the spell of the Nazis. Even Winston Churchill stated that had Hitler died before 1938 he would have been considered one of the greatest leaders in world history because of all that he had accomplished in rebuilding Germany. But the true nature of this diabolical leader was revealed, and many today still have trouble believing such a brilliant and cultured people as the Germans could have fallen to such depravity. The truth is that the same thing could happen at almost any time to any nation that remains ignorant of the enemy's schemes.

What does this have to do with us now? In 1990, several prophetic friends and I all received the same revelation that the very demonic powers that had seduced Germany had been sent to the United States to seduce our country. Because of this revelation, I have spent a considerable amount of time trying to understand what happened in Nazi Germany. I have been astonished by what I have learned and how true this revelation was. I will be writing a lot about this in the future, but it is my basic belief that when we are shown the schemes of the enemy, it is so we can thwart them. This will not be done just by writing articles or books. The church must begin to walk in the authority that we have been given over demonic forces on every level.

There is another great awakening coming to America. It is right at the door. With this outpouring of the Holy Spirit, the disguises of the evil one which are gripping so many in America and Europe, are going to be stripped away. As we read in the Book of Revelation, when the devil was cast out of heaven, his high place, he came to the earth with great wrath. This is going to stir up a lot of things we need to be prepared to deal with.

A Lesson From Hurricane Katrina

Katrina means "cleansing" or "to cleanse," and this hurricane was named right. It began a great spiritual cleansing of the Gulf Coast region. Though New Orleans has become known as "sin city" to many, we should not overlook that New Orleans and the Gulf Coast region have some great Christians, great churches, many great businesses, and great communities. We do tend to judge people and things by their most extreme elements, which is a basic deception. Even so, though they may still have a hard time understanding it, Katrina was the answer to the prayers of many Christians to clean up their region.

Though there were many upstanding people and churches there, New Orleans was a center for the occult and sexual perversion. When the people were scattered from New Orleans, there were reports of crime rising dramatically in places where the refugees went. Suddenly, there was an almost instant increase in demonic assaults on churches and church members. We had things happen that we had never experienced before, and it got our attention when those who were causing the problems were from New Orleans.

Some of those causing problems may have been involved in that kind of behavior before, but not necessarily. One basic thing we must learn about the schemes of the devil is that he uses traumatic experiences to gain entry into people's lives. Traumatized people do things that they would not normally do. Traumatized people can be much more open and subject to demonic control. As trauma increases around the world, this is something we must come to understand, and know how to take authority over.

We need also to keep in mind that after the people had been scattered from New Orleans, many communities were blessed with great people who quickly became a blessing instead of a burden. This disaster brought out the best in some and the worst in others. That is what we can expect in every catastrophe. We need also to understand that those who may be temporarily overcome with evil are not that way, and will not be that way for very long. We need to learn to overcome evil with good.

Even so, I know many felt that the devil had sent those with serious problems to attack their churches and people, and in fact, the devil himself may have felt that he was doing this, but the Lord was sending them to us to get set free. Some of those who may at first behave very badly can become some of the best neighbors and church members. However, we do need to know how to set them free from the things that may have a grip on them when they come.

The Lord's Best Friends

Here is the shocker—some of those who had the biggest problems, and maybe even were the most perverted, were sent to us to become pillars in our churches. Who was it that gathered around the Lord when He walked the earth, and who did He choose to be the future leaders of His church? He has not changed, and He is still building His church with the same kind of people.

The truly wise and experienced are more comfortable around those who are in the grip of demonic oppression than around those with a self-righteous religious spirit. The demonically-oppressed are probably much safer to be around spiritually and have in our churches than someone with a religious spirit. The demon-possessed would fall at Jesus' feet and beg for mercy, but the religious crucified Him. Those who were set free from their bondage, and who were forgiven of much tended to love Him much. Likewise, those who were forgiven of little tended to love Him little.

The people who come to us with serious problems, even demonic problems, can be far more beneficial to us and our churches in the long run than the prosperous, conservative, mature believers, who we usually tend to put our hope in. It will be the conservative and mature who are the most prone to become lukewarm, and then they are a much more serious problem than those who are presently cold toward the Lord.

Of course, this does not mean that those who are conservative and mature are all lukewarm. There are conservative, mature Christians who maintain their passion and fire for the Lord their entire lives, and can be pillars in the church. However, this is rare. This is why studies have shown that 98 percent of the Christians who lead others to the Lord do so in the first two years of their Christian walk. After two years in the faith, the overwhelming majority of Christians do not lead anyone else to the Lord. This is because after a couple of years most Christians begin losing their passion for the Lord, and therefore lose their passion for the lost that He gave His life to save.

Our goal should be maturity without losing the fire. However, the mature who are repelled by those in darkness instead of being devoted to liberating them are a worse enemy of the Gospel than those in blatant sin. Luke warmness is the worst state that any Christian could ever fall into, and even the Lord said that it would be better for one to be hot or cold, but the lukewarm He would spew out of His mouth (see Revelation 3:15-16). New believers are coming into our churches, especially those who have been delivered out of great darkness, can help to stir up the fires again in a way that no amount of preaching and teaching can.

Those Of True Value

We invest ourselves in people. If you want a good return on your investment with people, like any other investment, buy low and sell high. If you give yourself to helping those who are down, they will be your friends for life, but when you give yourself to someone who is already doing well, what reward should you expect for that?

Consider King David and his mighty men. The disgruntled, in debt, and other misfits were the ones who joined him when he was fleeing from Saul. However, these became the mighty men of Israel, the key leaders in the kingdom, and the king's friends for life, who loved David so much that some of them would even risk their lives just to get him a drink of water.

It is our basic mandate to help set the captives free. This is what we do. This is not just about investing in those who can benefit our churches or us, but for those whom the Lord so valued that He paid the highest price that could be paid for them—His own Son. Whether we even see a person again or not, we should treat them as this valuable.

Those in the grip of demonic bondage are loved so much by God that He gave His own Son for them, and these are the ones who will tend to love Him the most when they are set free. We must not see these people as problems sent to us by the devil, but as treasures sent to us by the Lord. When converted and set free, these will also tend to be the most faithful and fruitful.

Therefore, we need to view the situation, such as the many from New Orleans who had serious problems being scattered abroad, as an opportunity if they come to us. However, if we do not know our authority over demonic powers and use it, we are going to be in for some difficult times ahead.

Every Christian has authority over demons. No Christian should be intimidated by demons or demon-possessed people. If we run from this calling to set the captives free, we will soon be running all of the time. If this is something you do not want to get involved in and have resolved not to, you may as well change this mindset now because you will not escape the confrontation with demonic powers for much longer.

Give Them Spiritual Weapons

The newest Christian who has been given the Holy Spirit has more power and more spiritual authority in them than all of the power of the enemy. We have been given divinely powerful weapons. However, few understand them, and few have been equipped to use them. This must change. Those who do not understand and walk in this authority, and know how to use these divinely powerful weapons, will find themselves in increasingly difficult situations, and even jeopardy. The Lord gave us the armor and the weapons of our warfare because we need them.

Equipping comes after training. Training comes after teaching. Soldiers have to be taught about their weapons and then trained to use them before they are trusted with them. In general, the church has been stuck in the teaching mode, and we must go on to training and then equipping the saints to do the work of the ministry.

*This was written by Rick Joyner as a 2006 Special Bulletin found on the internet!

https://www.morningstarministries.org/resources/special-bulletins/2006/authority-over-demons#.V6TsXugrKUk

*3. The Amway Spirit (1978)

Is there a Spirit of Amway? NO! And yet so many times God's people are deceived by demonic spirits and circumstances that look favorable for them to make big money. I know one Spirit filled older couple who are very close to us, who told us they had been suckered into over nine multilevel marketing programs through the years. They informed us that they had never made any money, not even one time through these multilevel marketing schemes. People are sincere and excited about the business that they are launching off into completely convinced that it is God who sent this opportunity to them. They want you to be a part of this wonderful money making the opportunity to make money for the kingdom. They're completely convinced that this is God leading them and guiding them, not realizing it's simply the lust of their flesh. They want you to be a part of what they're involved in because first of all, they need your participation to build their team. Then they need you to build your team to get a residue of your sales, to make them successful.

Through the years many people have tried to get me involved in this kind of businesses. Thank God that 95% of the time they have not been able to sucker me in. In the spring of 1977 and evangelist friend and I walked into a music store in state college Pennsylvania. As we were talking to the owner of the store, there is a gentleman dressed in a three-piece suit who was in his early 30s who approached us. He wanted to know everything about our wonderful ministry in Mount Union PA. We shared with him about the work we were doing at our outreach ministry to the street people, drug users, low income community. He informed us that he would love to come and visit us with the next couple weeks. That he would like to even make some contributions to help us in our endeavors.

When we left the music store, I informed my coworker that there just wasn't something right with this man. I told him I perceive there is some kind of spirit that it was upon him, operating through him. As we were driving back to Mount Union PA, it's like a light came on inside of me. I told my coworker that I knew what spirit was operating in this man. He asked me what it was? I told him, **he's an Amway man**. He asked me what? I said this man was involved in Amway, and that he was going to come to see us to try to convince us to become a part of this multilevel marketing company.

Approximately one week later this man showed up at our ministry. He was extremely enthused about us, and in what we were endeavoring to do. He then informed us that he had a wonderful opportunity for us to fund our ministry. All he wanted was just a couple minutes of our time. We went into the office, with him carrying his briefcase. When he opened up his briefcase, he would not come out and tell us exactly what he was involved in. It was a hush-hush, very secret, very profitable business that he was going to invite us to be involved in. Sure enough: It Was Amway! He wanted us to be involved so bad, that he even paid for me to be a part of it. I informed him that I had no desire to do multilevel marketing. I could not convince him to leave us alone. Eventually, he disappeared over the horizon. Many people are more excited about making money with wonderful opportunities than they are about the gospel of Jesus Christ.

I wish I could say that I never got suckered into any of these schemes, but in 2005 though, I fell for one of these schemes, hook, line, and sinker. Not only did I fall for it, but I got my wife involved, my oldest son, members of our church, and other friends. Yes, like a dummy I was led like a sheep to the slaughter. And yes, we all lost our shirts. Please do not misunderstand me, I'm not saying that people cannot make a living off of these different endeavors. It's basically that you have to pour your whole life into trying to make them work. My purpose in life is not to get caught up in making money, but trying to win souls for Christ, and to see the captive set free. I find most people that get wrapped up in these schemes, are not looking truly at seeing people saved, but potential new representatives. Without really wanting to, they see a dollar sign written on your face.'

*4. Took Authority Over an Epileptic Seizure

My wife and I were at a building supply store (Lowes) doing some shopping, when all of a sudden, we noticed some commotion at the front of the store. It was at one of the checkout counters. The girl who had been working behind the counter had gone into an epileptic seizure. Everybody was just standing and staring at this girl as she fell to the ground kicking and squirming. Somebody was calling 9-1-1 to get help. A small crowd had gathered around the countertop, but nobody was trying to help her.

I'm the kind of guy who cannot be a spectator. So, I walked up. "Excuse me," I said, as I pushed my way through all of these people. I said, "Please, let me through, I am a doctor." This was the absolute truth, as I have a Ph.D. in biblical theology and a doctorate of divinity. I told the people standing there that I could help. I went over to the countertop, having to lean over it to see what was going on. This girl was on the floor thrashing away in a seizure. I simply leaned over the top of the counter, placed one hand on her arm. I whispered real quietly, "In the name of Jesus Christ of Nazareth, you lying devil lose her, and come out of her now!"

Immediately, her eyes stopped rolling; the convulsions stopped, and she came right up off of the floor. But when she stood up, it was not to thank me for helping her. She came up off the floor with a demonic snarl. She began to cuss and swear at me for taking authority over these demonic spirits. It could have become a brutal battle, but the Spirit quickened me to walk away. This was not the time or place. Plus, the Holy Ghost revealed to me that this girl had invited these demons into her life to draw attention to her. It saddens my heart how many people are embracing their infirmities, depressions, and oppressions to use them for their benefits, either in the form of sympathy or for financial gain.

*5. I was deceived by the devil (1984)

This is a very important story I have to tell. It may not seem important at first, but as you read this story, you'll discover that it is. In the spring of 1984, I was really hungry for God, wanting to draw closer to Him. To do this, I felt it was necessary for me to get alone with the Lord. So, I asked my wife if she would mind if I rented a room for a week at a rundown motel right down the road from our house; probably about a mile away. She said that would be fine with her and besides, she could visit me anytime that she wanted. With my wife's blessing, I packed up a little suitcase of clothes, got in my car and drove down to the motel to rent a room. After making arrangements, I moved in. In the room I had, there a large TV which I did not want to watch, so I unplugged it and turned the screen towards the wall. Then I sat down with my Bible, lexicons, concordances and notepads and began to study and pray. During the coming week, I had determined that I was going to do nothing but pray, seek God's face, fast and deny my flesh.

My motive in this would seem to be right, but there was something a little distorted in this quest. You see, I wanted to hear the voice of God, very precisely and explicitly. Now, you might ask what's wrong with that. At the time I did not realize it, but my motives were all wrong. Pride motivated me. If the great Dr. Michael Yeager could be used by God using the gifts of knowledge and wisdom, then people would be stunned with amazement; astounded and dumbfounded as to how God was using me.

You see, I had heard of and read about men that were so precise with their words of knowledge and wisdom that people would sit in complete and utter wonder at their abilities to know their problems and situations. I wanted what they had; all for the glory of God or so I told myself. But in all reality, my endeavor was all about me, me, and me. This is such an easy trap to fall into to truly believe that our goals are for the glory of God when, in all reality, it is for self.

Okay readers, back to the story which I was sharing. So here I was, locked up in this motel room, thinking that I was sincerely seeking the face of God when I was fully motivated by pride. I was doing everything right. I was praying, fasting, reading my Bible, memorizing scriptures and getting all pumped up. I knew the voice of God from almost a decade of walking with Him, but pride had crept in unaware and began to cloud my judgment. What I am sharing with you is extremely important because many well-known men of God have gone astray even, ending up believing that they were Elijah or some other famous prophet.

They heard a voice telling them something that was going to puff up their egos, their self-worth. A lot of the affirmation people are giving and preaching today is simply nothing more than the pumping up of the flesh, which ultimately leads to destruction and death. Our identity does not come from who we are or what we accomplish but who Jesus is in us. "In Christ" realities! It frightens me to ponder upon how much pride still dwells in my heart and the hearts of other ministers, because we can only take people where we are living. If I am egotistical, prideful, self-loving, self-serving and self-centered, then that is the only place where I can lead people.

So there I was, about the third day into this endeavor, when early in the afternoon I hear a voice in my mind telling me, "There is a pencil behind the desk." In my mind, I saw an image of a long, standard, yellow school pencil with an orange eraser at the top. Oh, how my heart got ever so excited thinking that God was going to begin to show me even simple little things. Wow, would people ever be impressed once I came out of this motel room being able to tell them what was even in their pockets. Now, for me to get behind this desk, I was going to have to move this very large television from off of it. The first thing that I did was move the chair out of the way; then I grabbed hold of this large, monstrosity of a television set; huffing and puffing, I moved it over to the bed, setting it down onto the mattress. The desk was rather large, so I walked to the side of it and grabbed it the best that I could, picking it up on one end and dragging it slowly away from the wall far enough to where I could get behind it. Then, I very excitedly got down on my hands and knees and began to look for this yellow pencil with an orange eraser.

But something was wrong. There was no pencil there. Surely it had to be there because I know the voice of God; I heard it. It was there. It had to be. I kept looking and looking for a very long time. High and low I kept on looking for this pencil that I knew God had shown me was there. I had become obsessed with finding this very special pencil because this was the foundation upon which I was going to begin to have a worldwide ministry. All of my success was built upon the fact that I must find that pencil.

All I can say is, thank God that I never did find that pencil! Now, why in the world would I say this? Because if I had found that pencil, it would not have been the Spirit of God speaking to me but a familiar spirit speaking to and deceiving me. After this incident, I cried out to the Lord asking Him why I could not find that pencil that He showed to me. That's when the Lord began to speak to me very strongly, revealing to me my haughty and prideful heart. He opened up my understanding to see that many men and women have been completely hornswoggled, deceived, even hoodwinked by the devil through the spirit of pride.

During my 40 years of ministry plus, I have seen person after person falls into this very trap which had been set for me by the enemy of my soul. Many really and truly believe that they are hearing the voice of God when, in fact, they are listening to familiar spirits. The doorway by which the enemy is coming in is through our hearts filled with pride. I cannot tell you how many times that I had heard people say, **"God told me"** when it was no more God then there are green, polka-dotted men and black and white striped women living on the moon. I have heard people say, God told me to leave my husband, God told me to leave my wife; God told me to leave my job; God told me that I am Elijah ...., etc. etc. etc. This is how all false religions and doctrines begin, by having a spirit of pride wanting to be special or more important than anyone else. It all goes back to the very root of sin, which is me-ism, I, I, I inflated to the utmost degree.

CHAPTER THREE

DR. LESTER SUMRALL THE EXORCIST!

Dr. Sumrall was an American Pentecostal pastor and evangelist who was ~~mildly~~ Mighty used of God and bring in deliverance to those who are demonized. (February 15, 1913 – April 28, 1996) **I had been ordained by Dr. Sumrall back in the 80s.** He used to come and speak for the church I pastored, plus he had spoken at the Bible college that my wife and I had attended in the 70s.

Dr. Sumrall was wonderfully used of God in the ministry of exorcism. You can still buy these books which are full of wonderful truths on Amazon. Dr. Sumrall did not mess around when it came casting out Devils. Some people spend hours and hours trying to get Devils out of people, but Sumrall would cast them out in very short periods of time.

(Lester Sumrall) In my travels in over one hundred nations of the world, I have repeatedly been asked questions regarding eschatology (the doctrine of the last or final things). Often it is a direct question regarding the reality and the functioning of satanic and demon powers. In many instances, I have found that the inquiring persons needed answers to some un usual phenomena which had occurred in their community or home. I find it quite baffling that people in what we term "heathen lands" know more about the negative forces of evil than many church people living in our Western civilization. Personally, I feel it is time for Christians to become acquainted with the unseen world of the spirit, both negative and positive. Much of our modern civilization is too materialistically minded. However, some scientists are coming to realize that there is a real world of the spirit, and they are delving into its mysteries at this present time. Also, multitudes of inquiring people are dabbling in Spiritism and other non-biblical cults. To counterbalance this activity, today's Christian must possess the positive power of God and be a living witness to the Spirit of God. The Apostle Paul was very strong to say that we are not ignorant of his (Satan's) devices (2 Cor. 2:11). You and I must not be ignorant of them either. The Lord Jesus wants His Church to set multitudes free. He said, *If the Son therefore shall make you free, ye shall be free indeed (John 8:36).*The purpose of this book is to reveal the true potential of the followers of Christ to set individuals, communities, or nations free from any evil force of the enemy. There has never been a time when people were so eager for the right answers. This is especially true in the realm of the unseen spirit world.(from his book: 101 questions and answers about Satan)

Lester Sumrall Did not have some "special anointing" for casting out demons that other Christians don not or cannot have!

He was simply baptized in the Spirit, and living in obedience, and in holiness as we are ALL supposed to be. Rooted and grounded in the Holy Word of God. Why is it that most Christians today pay little or no attention to this vital ministry of setting people free from the power of the devil? There has to be a reason. Please notice where Brother Sumrall encountered these demon spirits in people…it was in the very churches where he had gone to preach! Yes…evil spirits were and still are operating in churches, and not churches only, but even in believers and everywhere you go! Do not suppose that evil spirits simply disappeared or retired from their wicked agenda after Jesus went to be with the Father. Or, because you sit in church on Sunday with your Bible on your lap. Do not be so deceived my friends.

No, they are still active today, anywhere and everywhere they are given license to operate. If Christians aren't aware of this, they should be. Let me suggest that if Christians aren't aware and walking in the same power of the Holy Spirit that Brother Sumrall was, there is something lacking that the LORD not only wants us to have but that we SHOULD BE operating in. And it's all in His Word. Please! Read the gospels again, especially the gospel of Mark where Jesus did most of the casting out.

What would Jesus do? That silly powerless mantra that became popular some years back...Jesus would **CAST THEM OUT!** Now, He expects US to do it! Don't let anyone tell you this is not possible. It's not only possible...it's GOSPEL!

HOW LESTER SUMMERAL DEALT WITH DEVILS

Dr. Lester Sumrall years ago found himself in the middle of the Central American rain forest.

As he went about his ministry in that region, he came across a witch doctor. In today's rock and roll Hollywood scene, this witch doctor would look like a normal man … but, in those days, this was a pretty strange fellow!

In one hand, the witch doctor would hold a bull frog (always a symbol of Satanic power). In the other hand, a mixture of human blood and alcohol was placed in the frog's mouth. Then the witch doctor would dance, make satanic incantations and worship demon entities.

Fortunately, Dr. Sumrall wasn't raised in the modern-day school of humanistic, people-pleasing preachers. All Dr. Sumrall did was follow Jesus' biblical example. He placed his hands on the side of the witch doctor's head and said two words: **Come out!**

The witch doctor fell over with a thud. When he returned to his feet, the witch doctor was born again and speaking in a heavenly language and glorifying God.

Later, that night, Dr. Sumrall returned to his room to go to bed. Since it was warm, and without air conditioning, he decided to open the windows while he slept.

As he lay down, a strange odor began to fill the room. Suddenly, all of the sultry heat of the night disappeared from the room. A damp chill filled the place. It was so cold; Dr. Sumrall began to shiver. A wind began to blow the curtains wildly on their rods. Then, the bed began to shake so violently that it moved all the way out into the middle of the floor.

Well, Dr. Sumrall had enough of this! He raised up on his bed and said, "You demon spirit, I recognize you. I cast you out earlier today. In the name of Jesus Christ of Nazareth, you go now!"

Immediately, the evil presence left the room. The heat returned. The curtains laid down against the wall; the bed stopped shaking. The horrible odor left the room.

Now, most modern-day preachers would have written a book right there! They would have written seven books and told how the devil obeyed them … but, that wasn't Dr. Sumrall.

Instead, he rose back up in his bed, looked out the window and shouted, "Hey devil! Get back in here!

Immediately the curtains began to stick out on end as a wind rushed through the room. The coldness returned … the smell returned … the bed began to shake violently and almost shook him out of bed.

Dr. Sumrall sat up in his bed and said "Devil … When I came into this room, my bed was against that wall. **Now, in the name of Jesus, PUT IT BACK!"**

The bed went shaking back across the room and settled down against the wall.

"Now," Dr. Sumrall ordered, "get out of here!"

Most people will not believe a story like this, but I have personally experienced manifestations of evil spirits dealing in the physical realm. One of the major keys in dealing with Devils is that you never glorify them. **You never speak highly of them or exalt them.** So many of those who think they are called in to the deliverance ministry make a major mistake in this area. It is simply because they do not have faith in the God who created these entities and is so much greater than they are, that it is no big deal to cast them out. Listen to this amazing statement that Jesus made.

Luke 11:20 But if I with the finger of God cast out devils, no doubt the kingdom of God is come upon you.

Amazing Story of Lester setting Clarita Free!

Clarita Villanueva, a 17-year-old Filipina girl, had known a life of tragedy. She did not remember her father. She did not know if he had died or had deserted her mother.

Her mother was a spiritist and a fortune teller by vocation. The girl was brought up watching her mother holding séances, communicating with the dead, and using clairvoyance to predict to sinful people what they could expect in the future. Her mother took money from people for her services, and then laughed at them behind their backs. To her it was all just a game, a means of making a living by duping unsuspecting and gullible people.

When Clarita was still very young, about twelve years old, her mother died. Since she did not have any immediate family to take her in and care for her, she became a vagabond. She fell into the hands of harlots and at the tender age of 12 was selling her body as a prostitute. The harlots taught her how to handle men, how to get money for her services.

Clarita worked her way up from her island home to the capital city of Manila. The big city was a hiding place, a center of money and vice for her business. The local harlots became her teachers, and she learned the night life in the big capital city. In Manila, there were more men to seduce. By the time she was 17 years old, Clarita was frequenting the bars and taverns of Manila, living the 'gay life' by soliciting men for harlotry.

But one morning at two a.m. on the streets of down-town Manila, Clarita made the mistake of offering her services to a plainclothes police officer. The policeman called for a vehicle, and Clarita was taken to the ancient Bilibid Prison, used as the city jail. Bilibid has been a prison for over 300 years. The Spanish built it and used by the Americans, the Filipinos, and the Japanese as a prison and a place of torment.

Two days after Clarita was incarcerated, there struck the strangest phenomenon to ever hit Bilibid Prison in its 300-year history. This young harlot was bitten severely on her body by unseen and unknown alien entities. There were two of them – a huge monster-like spirit and a smaller one. They sunk their fangs and teeth deep into her flesh making deep indentations. They would bite her neck, back, legs and arms simultaneously. Blood flowed, mostly underneath her skin, from the bites. The 17-year-old girl screamed in horror and fainted.

The guards and medics heard the commotion and came running to the women's division of the prison. The other female inmates pointed to the writhing, tormented girl on a cot.

The girl was taken to the prison hospital for observation and treatment where all the doctors declared that they had never seen anything like it.

These strange demonic bitings began to occur daily, baffling all who saw it. Dr. Lara, the prison physician, appealed for help through the media and permitted many to view the strange phenomenon. Filipino, Chinese and American doctors, university professors, and other professionals were called in to analyze the situation.

The news media soon caught wind of the occurrence and sent reporters out to investigate. The newspapers, radio stations and magazines found it their kind of story and began to publicize it. Even the cartoonists were soon drawing pictures of the entities from Clarita's descriptions, as the biting's continued day by day. The UPI and other world news services began to report the phenomenon worldwide.

In my travels throughout the world, I have not been in any country in which the newspapers did not give this story front-page coverage. Switzerland, France, Germany, England, Canada, the United States – everywhere this strange phenomenon was front-page news at the time.

One doctor accused the girl of putting on an act in order only to get publicity. Clarita gazed at the doctor. With her snake-like eyes, she said: 'You will die.' He didn't feel anything at the moment, but the following day the doctor expired without even getting sick. He simply died. Fear struck the city when that news was spread about. The girl was not only a harlot; they said, she was also a witch who could speak curses upon human beings, and they would die.

The chief jailer had a confrontation with the girl. He had kicked her for something she had done wrong while rebelling against him. Clarita looked at the jailer in cold, inhuman hate and said: 'You will die!' Within four days the man was dead and buried, the second person to fall victim to her curse.

I walked into Bilibid Prison just as the funeral cortege moved out. The prison guards had paid their last respects to their chief. Dr. Lara, the chief medical officer, and his staff were deeply concerned. They had a prisoner who certainly was not crazy, but who was being wildly attacked by unseen entities and being bitten deeply on all parts of her body by creatures none else could see. I have never seen such a fearful and perplexed group of people as those I met in that prison that day. They were afraid that this thing would kill them as it had the two others who dared cross it. It was their responsibility to do something for the girl, yet they had no earthly idea what to do about the situation. It was beyond their medical knowledge.

Who were these alien entities? The large one, Clarita said, was a monster in size. He was black and very hairy. He had fangs that came down on each side of his mouth, plus a set of buck-teeth all the way around. The doctors verified her description by the teeth marks on her body: buck-teeth solid, all the way around the bite, rather than sharp teeth in the front.

The smaller entity was almost like a dwarf. He would climb her body to bite her upper torso. Both of these spirits liked to bite her where there was a lot of flesh, like the back of her leg, the back of her neck, the fleshy part of her upper arms. They would bite deep into her, leaving ugly, painful bruises.

Dr. Lara and his medical assistants called in all sort of observers, medical doctors, surgeons, psychiatrists and professors from the Far East University and the University of Santo Tomas. No one had ever witnessed such strange and demonic behavior. Nor did they know any solution to the problem. They all wondered who would be the next victim of her curse.

Dr. Lara and his staff sent out word everywhere: 'Come and help us. Please help us'. They received 3,000 cables from heathen countries suggesting possible cures, but not one from a Christian country.

Do you see how we Christians have been asleep? The word went out over the world. Three thousand telegrams came in, mostly from Japan and India, telling them what to do with an invisible biting monster. But not one Christian nation had any solution to the problem.

They asked in Manila for somebody to come and help. The only group who turned up were the spiritists who said it was John the Baptist biting her. The officials asked the spiritists to leave.

I was the next one to come upon the scene. After three awful weeks of this torture, a radio reporter came to Bilibid and taped a session while the doctors were violently struggling with the demonized harlot. The reporter immediately released his story on a local radio station, just after the 10 o'clock news.

This was the first I had heard of the hell in Bilibid Prison. The newspapers had given it front-page coverage, but I was too busy building a church to read the newspapers. That's what the devil would like for us to do, to get so involved in taking care of our little mission that we allow him a free rein to do anything he wants to do.

When the Bible says to be vigilant, this is what it means; to see what the devil is doing in the world; to keep up with him; to resist him and fight him in whatever he might be doing.

I stayed up all night praying and weeping before the Lord. I was interceding for the city, for the girl and myself. I was living in a city that had a great need, and I was not helping to meet that need. I was so busy putting up our church building and doing my own thing that I was not involved in the tragedy of Bilibid. The next morning God spoke to me and told me to go to that prison and pray for the demonized girl. I did not want to go, but God assured me that He had no one else in the city to send. Therefore I went.

Because I was a foreigner in the Philippines, I went to the mayor's office and asked permission to see Clarita. He granted me his permission but warned me that several people had been injured by the girl and that two had been cursed and were dead. I went with the understanding that I would not sue the government if I were hurt and that I would not complain if mistreated.

When I arrived at the prison, the head doctor of six physicians, Dr. Lara, was skeptical of this foreign minister, but he finally permitted me to see the girl.

Clarita was brought into a special room where I was waiting with a large group of news reporters, foreign members of the press, university professors, and medical doctors, who had been invited by Dr. Lara.

As Clarita was being led into the room, she looked at them and said nothing, but when she saw me she screamed violently: 'I hate you!' Instantly I inserted: 'I know you hate me. I have come to cast you out'.

That was the beginning of the confrontation. There was a raging battle with the girl blaspheming God the Father, God the Son, and God the Holy Spirit. Her eyes were burning coals of fire and full of hate. I commanded the evil spirit to lose her. After a three-day confrontation with the devil in her, the miracle of God came upon her. She relaxed, smiled, and said: 'He's gone.'

'Where did he go?' I asked.

'He went out that way,' she replied. 'He's gone.'

The local newspapers, magazines, and radio told the story. One headline read: 'He dies; the devil is dead!' Another one said: 'Devil loses round one.'

Dr. Lara became so excited he took me over to the office of the mayor. When he walked into the office, he said: 'My God, mayor. The devil is dead'.

I said: 'Mr. Mayor, Dr. Lara may be a good doctor, but he's a poor theologian. The devil is not dead. The girl I came and talked to you about yesterday is healed'.

From: Lester Sumrall, Alien Entities. A look behind the door to the spirit realm, printed in the USA by Whitaker House (PA), 1995, pages 131-138.

*6. Woman healed who was bent over & legally blind, (2015)

A brother brought his wife who was legally blind, and crippled. On Sunday night the spirit of God had come upon his wife, and she ran for the 1st time in 3 years. Plus God had restored some of her eyesight. Last night (midweek service) when he brought her I could tell there was a drastic difference in her walking, in her countenance, even her eyes were not near as dim. She informed me that she did not even need her walking cane anymore. The night before she had come and was bent over, but tonight she was standing straight up.

I ministering on the subject of signs, wonders, and miracles last night. When I was done, I called everybody up front. As I was ministering the word an praying for her, the Holy Ghost was all over her again. She was filled with great joy and began to bounce up and down, up and down, up and down! We didn't know exactly what was making her so excited, but maybe the Holy Ghost, but then she informed us that she could see the letters upon the wall which was probably 20 or 30 feet away from her. She was such a bubbly fountain of joy that some of us began to get drunk in the Holy Ghost. Once again I had her run by faith without any assistance. I did stand by her side a little, but she did wonderfully. It's a progressive healing, and she's getting better day by day.

As I anointed people's hands with oil there began to be an increase. The one precious sister who I'm sure is reading this needs a miracle in her body from a car accident. I put a little bit of oil on her hand next to her thumbs, the next thing we knew as we were watching, both hands were covered with oil. We all stood there in amazement as God manifested his glory through the increase of oil. I gave her a prophetic word that stated God was doing this to encourage her in her faith, and not to let go. That God was seeing her strong declaration that she was healed no matter how she felt. This Is the Faith that Pleases God!

*7. Instant deliverance from alcohol (1993)

I actually would rather have this precious sister tell her story, but because she is not here, I'll try my best to tell as much as I know about what happened to this sister in Christ in this particular service.

The summer of 1993 I was conducting a regular church service at our church in Gettysburg Pennsylvania. I noticed that we had a good handful of visitors that morning, including one particular lady who stood out above the rest because she was rather tall with dark hair. She looked like she was in her early to mid-30s. As I was preaching the word of God, I could see that the spirit of God was coming on her in a wonderful way, plus others.

After the message, I gave an altar call for those who needed to get right with God or needed a touch of the Holy Ghost. I still remember to this day, this particular lady coming forward for prayer. Before I even got a chance to pray for her, she began to shake under the power of the Holy Ghost. Something dramatic was happening to her by the spirit of God. I finally stood in front of her, laying my hands on her gently in the name of Jesus Christ of Nazareth.

I never, ever put pressure on people's heads when I pray for them. Some ministers I have watched put so much pressure on people's heads to where they're pushing them backwards. There are also ministers that I know who use their faith to get people to fall, thinking this is what they need, and it is a sign of God's presence. I never do this, because it's not the position of the body that matters to me, but what God is doing in their heart. I have seen people supernaturally touched in a powerful way, walking away transformed without ever falling under the power of God.

Now in this particular situation, I barely touched this sisters head when she just crumpled to the floor. She laid on the floor under the power of the Holy Ghost, shaking and quivering from head to toe. I moved on to the next person, never realizing until about fifteen years later what happened that day. This precious sister became a member of our church, with her sister and other members of the family.

It was about fifteen years later that my family and I were over at her family's house celebrating Thanksgiving together. As I was speaking to her about her life, she informed me what happened that day. Someone had invited her to our church service, and she came under the gentle urging of the spirit. Unbeknownst to me she was an alcoholic. She informed me that even when she came that Sunday morning, she had already been drinking. She was standing there in our church service drunk under the influence of alcohol. As I was preaching, the Spirit of God began to move on her in a wonderful way. When I gave the altar call, she could not help but come to the front to be prayed for. The power of the Holy Ghost came on her in a mighty way. She found herself laying on the floor. Right then and there the Holy Ghost completely delivered her from alcoholism.

She informed me on that Thanksgiving Day fifteen years later that from that moment, she never drank another drop. Thank God for the Holy Ghost, and the wonderful delivering power of the name of Jesus. The unclean spirit for the desire of alcohol had come out of her the minute hands were laid upon her!

*8. Why Did Lucifer Fall? (God asked me)

Today's Church is Making the Same Mistake Lucifer Did!

As I was standing in our kitchen early one Sunday morning getting ready to minister, out of the blue the Spirit of God spoke to me asking a very specific question. The Lord said to me, why did Lucifer fall? The voice of the Lord was so loud it seemed almost audible! It took me a while to respond because I was shocked to hear his voice at that moment. When I did respond I said to the Lord, Lucifer wanted to be God. But the Lord was not satisfied with my answer, and He asked me again. Why did Luci-fer fall? I responded with the same answer once again. A third time the Lord asked me again. Why did Lucifer fall? I finally realized that my answer was not correct, and I said, Lord, I do not know why! Lord, Please tell me why? His answer shocked me because I had never thought about it. This is what he said to me. Creation and the angelic realm of heaven had never seen my wrath, my anger, and my indignation. They have never seen me pouring out my punishment and wrath. All they had ever known was my goodness and blessings. They never had in their hearts seen me as a consuming fire. Then he said something even more shocking to me!

He said to me, this generation is making this same tragic mistake that the Angels made, and Noah's generation made. They proclaim that I am love, and this is true, but the fear of the Lord has departed from them. They did not believe and acknowledged my wrath, my anger, and my in-dignation against all ungodliness and wickedness. But they are about to experience this unless they repent.

CHAPTER FOUR

Where You Must Live to Cast Out Devil's!

This is a quick explanation of how to live and move in the realm of Divine Authority and Power. Demonic powers obeying you is not something that just spontaneously happens because you have been born-again. There are certain biblical principles and truths that must be evident in your life. This is a very basic list of some of these truths and laws:

1. **You must give Jesus Christ your whole heart.** You cannot be lackadaisical in this endeavour. Being lukewarm in your walk with God is repulsive to the Lord. He wants 100% commitment. Jesus gave His all; now it is our turn to give our all. He loved us 100%. Now we must love Him 100%. Demonic powers automatically know if you are Living in this realm!

My son, give me thine heart and let thine eyes observe my ways (Proverbs 23:26).

So then because thou art lukewarm, and neither cold nor hot, I will spew thee out of my mouth (Revelation 3:16).

2. **There must be a complete agreement with God's Word.** We must be in harmony with the Lord in our attitude, actions, thoughts, words, and deeds. Whatever the Word of God declares in the New Testament is what we wholeheartedly agree with. This is the realm of **FAITH!**

Can two walk together, except they are agreed? (Amos 3:3).

1 John 5:4 For whatsoever is born of God overcometh the world: and this is the victory that overcometh the world, even our faith. 5 Who is he that overcometh the world, but he that believeth that Jesus is the Son of God?

For the eyes of the LORD run to and fro throughout the whole earth, to shew himself strong in the behalf of them whose heart is perfect toward him (2 Chronicles 16:9).

3. **Obey and do the Word from the heart, from the simplest to the most complicated request or command.** No matter what the Word says to do, do it! Here are some simple examples: Lift your hands in praise, in everything give thanks, forgive instantly, gather together with the saints, and give offerings to the Lord, …etc.

   I can of mine own self do nothing: as I hear, I judge: and my judgment is just; because I seek not mine own will, but the will of the Father which hath sent me (John 5:30).

4. **Make Jesus the highest priority of your life.** Everything you do, do not do it as unto men, but do it as unto God.

   If ye then be risen with Christ, seek those things which are above, where Christ sitteth on the right hand of God. Set your affection on things above, not on things on the earth (Colossians 3:1-2).

5. **Die to self! The old man says, "My will be done!"** The new man says, "God's will be done!"

   I am crucified with Christ: nevertheless I live; yet not I, but Christ liveth in me: and the life which I now live in the flesh I live by the faith of the Son of God, who loved me, and gave himself for me (Galatians 2:20).

   Now if we be dead with Christ, we believe that we shall also live with him (Romans 6:8).

6. Repent the minute you get out of God's will—no matter how minor, or small the sin may seem. Give no place to the devil.

> *Revelation 3:19 As many as I love, I rebuke and chasten: be zealous therefore, and repent.*

7. Take one step at a time. God will test you (not to do evil) to see if you will obey him. *Whatever He tells you to do: by His Word, by His Spirit, or within your conscience, do it.* He will never tell you to do something contrary to His nature or His Word!

> *For whosoever shall do the will of my Father which is in heaven, the same is my brother, and sister, and mother (Matthew 12:50).*

> *Then went he down, and dipped himself seven times in Jordan, according to the saying of the man of God: and his flesh came again like unto the flesh of a little child, and he was clean (2 Kings 5:14).*

8. Never Exalt the Devil. You never exalt or boast on what the devil is doing. When you do that you're actually in your heart and mind saying that the enemy is greater than God. Jesus has already defeated the enemy, and this must be a reality in your heart.

Philippians 2:9 Wherefore God also hath highly exalted him, and given him a name which is above every name:10 That at the name of Jesus every knee should bow, of things in heaven, and things in earth, and things under the earth;11 And that every tongue should confess that Jesus Christ is Lord, to the glory of God the Father.

Colossians 2:15 And having spoiled principalities and powers, he made a shew of them openly, triumphing over them in it.

*9. Stabbed by a demon possessed ~~women~~!

*w*omen

I drove my motorcycle to Oregon, visiting a good friend of mine, Judge Lloyd Olds and his family. While I was there, I ended up working on a fishing vessel. Then I drove my motorcycle up the Alcan Freeway, caught a ferry to Alaska, and finished driving to Anchorage.

After I had arrived in Anchorage, it was quickened in my heart to stop at a small full gospel church that I used to visit. It just so happened that an evangelist I had known while I was in the Navy on Adak, Alaska, was there. We spent some time reminiscing what had happened the previous year. He shared how the Lord had laid upon his heart to go to Pennsylvania to open up an outreach center in a place called Mount Union, Pennsylvania. He invited me to go to Pennsylvania with him and his wife to open this evangelistic outreach. I perceived in my heart I needed to go with them. I planned to fly back to Wisconsin where he and his wife would pick me up as they went through. However, before I left Alaska, the spirit of God had one more assignment for me: a precious woman needed to be set free.

One Sunday we decided to attend a small church along the road to Fairbanks. I was the 1st to enter this little, old rustic church. When I went through the sanctuary doors, I immediately noticed a strange, little elderly lady across from me sitting in the pews. She turned her head and stared at me with the strangest look I have ever seen. I could sense immediately there was something demonic about her. Out of the blue, this little lady jumped up, got out of the pew, and ran out of the church. At that moment I perceived that God wanted me to go and cast the Devils out of her.

After the service, I asked the pastor who the elderly lady was who ran out of the service. He said she was not a member of his church, but she came once in a great while. He said she and her husband lived in a run-down house on a dirt road. I asked if it would be okay to go and see her. He said he had no problems with this, especially since she wasn't a part of his church. We followed the directions the pastor gave us.

When we arrived at this lady's house, we found it exactly as the pastor had said. It was a rundown house with its yard overflowing with old furniture and household items. The house reminded me of a TV show called "Sanford and Sons "but probably had ten times more junk in the yard. I do not know how they could survive the winters in Alaska in such a poorly-built house. As we got out of the car, a little old man met us outside. It was her husband. He was thanking God as he walked toward us and said he knew we were men of God and had been sent by the Lord to help his poor tormented wife. He informed us that his wife was in their kitchen.

We went to the house having to go down the twisting cluttered junk filled path. We entered through a screen door that led into their summer kitchen. When we entered the kitchen, we could see his wife over at a large utility sink. Her back was to us, but we could see she was peeling carrots over her kitchen sink with a very large scary butcher knife. I began to speak to her about Jesus. As I stood there looking at the back of her head out of the blue, she turned her head like it was on a swivel to look at me. I could hardly believe my eyes; it was like I was watching a horror movie! This little lady's eyes were glowing red on her swiveled head. I rubbed my eyes at that moment thinking that maybe I imagined this. But no, her head had swiveled without her body moving, and her eyes were glowing red. Fear immediately filled my heart as she looked at me with the big knife, a butcher's knife in her hand. Immediately I came against the spirit of fear in my heart quoting the Scripture *"God has not given me the spirit of fear, but of power love and a sound mind."*

I began to share with her about Jesus Christ. The next thing I knew she was coming right at me with her knife as if she was filled with great rage. The knife was still in her right hand when she spun around and came at me. She leapt through the air onto me wrapping her small skinny legs around my waist. How in the world she was able to do this, I do not know. The next thing I knew she was lifting her right hand and hitting me in the face very hard multiple times. I could feel the pressure of her hitting me on the left side of my face. As she was hitting me in the face out of my mouth came **In the Name of Jesus!**

The minute I came against this attack in **The Name of Jesus**, she was ripped off of me, picked up by an invisible power and flew across the room about 10 feet or more. She slammed very hard against the bare wall of her kitchen and slipped down to the floor. Amazingly when she hit the wall, she was not hurt. I went over to her continuing to cast the demons out of her **In the Name of Jesus**. Once I perceived that she was free and in her right mind, I asked her how she had become demon possessed? She told us her terrible story.

Her uncle had repeatedly molested and raped her when she was a very young girl. She thought she was free from him when he got sick and had died. But then he began to visit her from the dead, continuing to molest and rape her at night. To her, it was physical and real. She did not know it was a familiar spirit disguised as her uncle. This probably had gone on for over 50 years. I led her to the Lord. Sweet, beautiful peace came upon her, completely changing her countenance. She was a brand-new person in Christ, finally free after almost 50 years of torment. She and husband began to go to church with us until I left Alaska. I remember that we took them to see the Davis family who was at a local church visiting Alaska as a missionary trip.

Years later the evangelist who was with me heard me retell this story at a church about how this woman kept punching me forcefully with the right hand. After the end of the service, he came to me informing me that I was not telling this story correctly. I wondered if he thought I was exaggerating. He said that he was standing behind me when she jumped on top of me and began to hit me with her right fist. But he informed me that it wasn't her hand she was slapping me with, but that she still had the large butcher knife in her hand, and he saw her stabbing me in the face with this knife repeatedly. He said he knew that I was a dead man because nobody could survive being stabbed in the face repeatedly with a large butcher knife. He expected to see nothing but blood, but instead of seeing my blood everywhere he saw that there was not even one mark on my face from where the knife was hitting me. I did feel something hit my face, but I thought it was her hand. Instead, it was her knife, and it could not pierce my skin! Thank God for his love, His mercy, and as supernatural divine protection.

I am convinced that if I had not been walking with God in his holiness and obedience the devil in that little lady with a stab me to death. Many people in the body of Christ are trying to deal with demonic powers when they are out of the father's will. When we are moving in the Holy Ghost, obedience, absolute love for Jesus Christ there is no power in hell that can hurt us.

*10. A Brothers Imagination was Out of Control!

We must bring our imaginations into captivity. We dare not let our imaginations run wild. Every imagination that is not brought under the control of the authority of God will become a playground for the devil. There is a brother who comes to our church in a spasmodic fashion, and yet he has been coming here for years. Now this particular brother is extremely paranoid. In his imagination, he thinks that everybody is plotting against him., and that there is a spy behind every corner. He came to me a short time ago, asking me in a whisper exactly how many people have come to me to talk about him. I asked him if he was referring to all the year's sense I have known him. (It has been probably seven years when he first showed up at our church). Yes, he told me, he wanted to know how many times people had come to me about him, and who exactly it was that had asked these questions? I asked him once again: are you sure you want to know? Yes, he excitedly said.

Okay, I told him that there had not been even one person in all of these years who had ever come to me, called me, or asked me about any information about him. He seemed in complete and total shock. He said: really? I said: Absolutely, no one has ever said one word to me about you. You see, here is a born again, spirit filled man who was allowed the enemy to mess with his imagination. How many people's lives are destroyed because they have not brought their imaginations into captivity with the word of God.

The Bible says that God had to destroy all living creatures in the days of Noah because the imaginations of men were nothing but continually evil.

Genesis 6:5 And God saw that the wickedness of man was great in the earth and that every imagination of the thoughts of his heart was only evil continually.

The imaginations of our mind are like a wood stove fire. The only way that the fire will keep burning is if you keep feeding it fuel. It's the same thing with our imaginations. The Scripture says: as a man think of so is he. We could also say that the imagination of the mind of a man will determine what kind of man he becomes. Nobody who is a murderer, rapist, adulterer, or any other type of evil person started out that way. They began with a twisted corrupt seed in the imagination of their minds. They kept on feeding that seed until it germinated and sank its roots deep into every part of their lives.

That imagination took them over, bringing death and destruction where ever they went. For the fire of this twisted thought to go out, you need to use the water of the word to douse it. The divine weapons of our warfare are more than sufficient to overcome these demonic imaginations. David gave to his son Solomon this solemn warning that God knows all of the imaginations and the intents of the heart.

*11. I have demons - not! (1976)

At 19 years old, I was working in a rustic town by the name of Dillingham, Alaska. I was a 19-year-old kid who was trying to evangelize the Yupik Indians and anybody else I could reach. All summer and into the fall I worked, fished and lived side-by-side with not just those in Dillingham but with other natives from other villages. This little town has become famous now because of Sarah and Todd Palin who go there every season to fish for salmon. When I was in this town back in 1975 to 1976, it was a rough-and-tumble world. Dillingham was nothing but dirt roads, rustic buildings and hardy Alaskans with strapped pistols at their sides, walking around with rifles like it was still the old rugged West. I was dressed in like fashion with a .357 Magnum at my side, a .270 Winchester rifle slung over my shoulder, wolf mukluks on my feet for the winter and a silver-fox, hooded coat to complete the ensemble.

Right outside the town of Dillingham, there is what was commonly called "The Mud Flats." It is an area that many natives would set their tents up to live and work from during the salmon season. At that time, I was living in a makeshift shack right outside of town on these mud flats. It was traditionally only a summertime place for those who were fishing to set up a temporary residence. Everybody had left it a long time before except for me. I had nowhere else to stay. The winter had come before I knew it. After summer, with some help, I covered a tent with plywood on the outside and with thin insulation and plywood on the inside. We had found a big old bay window with only single-paned glass and installed it in the back portion of the tent. This window faced the Nushagak River upon which Dillingham was built next to. This is where all the boat docks were located, close to the cannery.

Dr Michael H Yeager

I got myself an old 55 gallon barrel and put a wood stove pipe on one end and a door on the other where I could insert wood. To support myself during the wintertime, I applied for a job at one of the only gas stations at that time. They hired me to pump gas, change tires and do grunt work as required.

Before I knew what happened, winter came with her full Arctic vengeance. I'm telling you it was one cold and snowy winter. In my plywood covered tent, the wind would shake it as it blew across the mud flats. It was over 50° below outside not counting the wind-chill factor. My bed was nothing but a wooden frame with a piece of plywood. I would crawl into my sleeping bag praying and believing God that I would not freeze during the night. I would get up the next morning to walk 5 miles to work. Over 90% of the time, I would never get a ride. My heart was content; however, as I would cry out to Jesus, I would ask Him for the opportunity to share the good news with anyone I met or who would listen to me. My heart yearned to win souls and to be more like Jesus every day. This cry has never left me. Here was an environment that would try the hearts and test the faith of any godly man. I want you to know that God was with me in a powerful way in this situation.

So here I was, living on the howling, freezing, lonely Mud Flats. Nobody else was there but me and Jesus. One extremely cold morning, I got up freezing. My mustache was covered with frost from my breath. I was so cold that I knew that I needed to start a fire real quick. What I did next, I knew better but at the time it didn't concern me. I had some gasoline which I kept to help start fires. I took an old coffee can and filled it probably half-full. After I had the wood stove full of wood, I threw the gasoline onto the logs. Then I took a match and threw it into the 55 gallon drum. Of course, you know what happened. It exploded, sending fire rushing out of the barrel and engulfing me head to toe! The blast was so huge that it threw me onto my back. In spite of my stupidity, God protected me. I had some singed hair on my face and head, but that was the only damage.

What unforgettable and amazing adventures I had during that time of my life! I look back now and am utterly amazed at how God kept me and preserved me during those times. Thank you, Jesus, for Your wonderful protection and mercy!!!

Isaiah 43:2 When thou passest through the waters, I will be with thee; and through the rivers, they shall not overflow thee: when thou walkest through the fire, thou shalt not be burned; neither shall the flame kindle upon thee.

I was still living on the mud flats right outside of Dillingham, Alaska. During this time, I did not know any other true believers. I'm not saying that there weren't any in Dillingham, I'm just saying that I did not know of any. I was striving to live for God. I do not remember how or by whom, but a book came to me. This little book has become famous in the modern day church dealing with the subject of believers having demons.

As I read this book it began to tell me that every manifestation of the flesh in my life was because demons possessed me. At the time I was not very deep in the word of God.

Actually, I was hoping that this teaching was correct because then the wrong desires within my mind and my heart were not me but demons. This book said that I needed deliverance; I simply had to cast them out. I mean, I swallowed this doctrine hook, line, and sinker. (By the way, I am not saying that Christians cannot have demons because I have cast them out of believers through the years.)

So, I began to take authority over all of these demons in my life, my body, my mind and my emotions that were giving me so many problems and commanding them to come out of me **In Jesus Name**. This book said that every time demons would leave you, it would be manifested by hiccups, burping or the release of other kinds of gas. I'm not kidding you. So, during this time in my life, every time that I burped, hiccupped, or passed gas; I thought demons were leaving me. LOL--- I am not kidding!

For a while, I believed that I was getting somewhere. I did not know that a born again, a spirit-filled believer could have so many devils but I was soon to discover that it was all an illusion, a deception —a dead end road. These works of the flesh kept creeping back into my life every time I turned around no matter how many times that I cast the "demons" out. Or, so I thought. Actually, I'm sorry to say that for a very brief time I became more devil conscious, then Jesus conscious. This is what this kind of false teaching does. It takes your mind and eyes off of Jesus Christ and puts them upon the devil, and manifestations.

I then discovered, by reading the Bible, that the scriptures required me to be transformed by the renewing of my mind (Romans 12:2). I am to take captive every thought and subject it to obedience unto Christ. God also requires me to present my body as a living sacrifice; holy and acceptable unto God.

Romans 12:1I beseech you therefore, brethren, by the mercies of God, that ye present your bodies a living sacrifice, holy, acceptable unto God, which is your reasonable service.2 And be not conformed to this world: but be ye transformed by the renewing of your mind, that ye may prove what is that good, and acceptable, and perfect, will of God.

2 Corinthians 10:3 For though we walk in the flesh, we do not war after the flesh:4 (For the weapons of our warfare are not carnal, but mighty through God to the pulling down of strong holds;)5 Casting down imaginations, and every high thing that exalteth itself against the knowledge of God, and bringing into captivity every thought to the obedience of Christ;

I have been given the power of choice. I can choose to submit to God and to resist the devil, knowing that he will flee from me. I am not attacking the whole deliverance ministry because there are people who are demonically oppressed, possessed and depressed, and obsessed. I am simply saying that a lot of our issues are not going to be resolved by a one-time declaration of commanding the devils to go.

We must seek God, renew our mind, submit to and obey the gospel of the Lord Jesus Christ, resist the devil, take up our cross and follow Christ! Believe me; I have made tremendous progress by meditating upon God's word night and day. So now when I burp, hiccup or pass gas; I know that it's not demons. I simply ate something that did not agree with my stomach.

2 Corinthians 2:11lest Satan should get an advantage of us: for we are not ignorant of his devices.

Too Many Believers Are Spiritual Pacifist

When the enemy comes in like a flood, if I will trust God, act upon the word, God will raise up a standard against the enemy. I'm amazed at how many believers are such pacifist when it comes to fighting the off the enemy by Faith in Christ. You have to rise up in the name of **Jesus Christ and speak against that circumstance which is contrary to God's will**. If the circumstance does not seem to change, you do not let go of having a heart that is thankful and worshipful towards the Lord. Here is an illustration in my personal life.

The other day I was lying in bed all night long with terrible pain racking my body, yet I am fighting the fight of faith, speaking the Word, and praying quietly as I'm lying in bed. I never allow a spirit of fear to control and dictate my actions. The next thing I know my left hand went completely numb with my fingers all curled up. The devil said to me: you're having a stroke. Immediately jumped out of bed, and I took my numb left arm with its curled up fingers and began to beat it against my right hand commanding it to be healed. I knew that this circumstance was not of God because **by his stripes we were healed**! I had to rise in the spirit of faith speaking to this circumstance in and by the **Name of Jesus**.

After over 40 years of practice, I know in most situations what is, and what is not the will of God. After I had commanded my arm and my hand, my body to be healed, I began to thank the Lord that it was done. Now, in the natural my arm and my hand was still in the same condition as it was before I spoke to it in the **name of Jesus**, but I know that **God Cannot Lie**. Praise the Lord, within a short period of time my left arm and hand was completely restored, and all the pain left my body. This took place back in about 2009. We should never give into the lie, or the symptoms that the enemy is trying to use against us. The minute the enemy sticks his ugly head up, we need to cut it off with the word of God.

When I was a kid, we used to fish in a favorite fishing hole. It was filled with pan fish, crop-pies, and blue gills. The only problem is that it also had lots of mud turtles. These nasty turtles would kill anything that was in their path. Whenever we went fishing, we would always carry our 22 rifles. When these mud turtles stuck their heads up, we popped them with our 22 rifles. We were not going to allow them to devour the fish we were trying to catch. If we had not done this, there would have been no fish left in this pond. It is the same way spiritually. You cannot allow the devil, and is demonic host to simply run over you. We must rise up, and overcome spiritual pacifism.

Psalm 119:71 It is good for me that I have been afflicted; that I might learn thy statutes.

Romans 8:14 For as many as are led by the Spirit of God, they are the sons of God.

James 4:7Submit yourselves therefore to God. Resist the devil, and he will flee from you.

CHAPTER FIVE

Can a Christian Be Possessed?

Written by: John Eckhardt

There was a time when we taught in our church that Christians could not have demons. I preached long sermons stating that Christians could be oppressed, regressed, digressed, obsessed and suppressed, but never possessed. We believed that a demon could be outside a Christian oppressing him but that it could not be inside him. The reasoning I used to defend this position was that Jesus and the Holy Spirit could not live inside the same body in which demons reside.

The problem was, our experience did not match our theology. When we ministered deliverance, we frequently prayed for people we knew born-again, Spirit-filled believers--and they manifested demons! We had to face the fact that either our experience was wrong or our doctrine was wrong.

We couldn't question our experience because we knew what we were seeing. So we began to question our theology. In our search for truth, we realized that in the Bible, Jesus tells us to cast devils out, not to cast devils off. Obviously, for something to come out, it must be in. We finally came to the conclusion that our interpretation of the Bible had been wrong.

Now I am convinced not only that a Christian can have demons but also that there are demons that operate in the realm of theology, encouraging us to argue and debate endlessly over doctrine rather than meeting the needs of people who are hurting.

Demons help promote the teaching that a Christian cannot have a demon because they gain strength from staying hidden. They can operate in their destructive ways without being challenged!

Some may argue that a believer cannot be possessed. But the dismaying fact remains that born-again Christians, including leaders, are experiencing difficulties that can find no solution in natural infirmities or the endless conflict between the flesh and the Spirit.

It's time to acknowledge that we are dealing with real people who have real problems and that God did not save and commission us so we could argue over doctrine. He called us into ministry so we can help people who are hurting, wounded and bruised.

When you come into contact with someone who is controlled by demons, the answer is to cast the devils out, not to argue about whether or not the person is a Christian. The answer is to bring help to that person.

Possessed or Not Possessed?

I realize I'm not the only believer who has ever had an erroneous idea about Christians being possessed. And the sensationalized picture Hollywood has painted of demon possession has not helped. It has led us to believe that if we say a Christian can be possessed, we are saying he can be fully owned and controlled by the devil and will manifest, Hollywood-style, with head spinning and eyes popping out.

The word "possessed" is an unfortunate translation because it connotes ownership, and we know that the devil cannot own a Christian--that is, have complete control of him. But in the Bible, there is no real distinction between being possessed and being oppressed, digressed, suppressed, obsessed and so forth. All these terms mean that a person is, to some degree, under the influence of a demon.

Personally, I do not have as much of a problem with the word "possessed" as other Christians do. In fact, to me the word "demonized" sounds worse.

When I looked up "possess" in the dictionary, I discovered that one definition of the word is "to occupy." My contention is that if a demon occupies your big toe, he possesses that part of you. It doesn't mean he possesses your spirit, soul, and body. But if he occupies even a small portion, such as a physical organ in your body--as a spirit of infirmity does--then there is possession to some degree.

I often ask those who are skeptical of demon possession whether or not cancer is demonic. Most will agree that sickness is of the devil.

So then, I continue, is cancer inside the body, or is there something on the outside that's the problem? If it isn't on the inside, doctors probably won't cut people open trying to remove it. Evidently, as a Christian, you can have something in you that is possessing a certain organ of your body and is not of God.

Knowing that a Christian can be possessed (or demonized) in some part of his being raises the question: Is any part off-limits to demons? Here is where we can reconcile the issue of Jesus and the Holy Spirit residing simultaneously within someone who needs deliverance.

One thing that has helped us in our understanding is the realization that every person is made up of three parts: spirit, soul, and body. When Jesus comes into a believer's life, He comes into that person's spirit. John 3:6 tells us clearly, "That which is born of the Spirit is spirit" (NKJV). A demon cannot dwell in a Christian's spirit because that is where Jesus and the Holy Spirit dwell.

It is the other components that make up a human being--the soul (mind, will and emotions) and the body--that are the targets of demonic attack. Demons can dwell in those areas of a Christian's life. So when we say that a Christian is demonized or possessed, we are not saying he has a demon in his spirit but in some part of his soul or body.

To illustrate this truth, the Lord reminded us of the biblical account of Jesus' going into the temple and cleansing it of thieves and moneychangers. The Greek word used for "drove out" in this account is ekballo, which means "to expel or drive out." It is the same word that is used in Mark 16:17: "In My [Jesus'] name they will cast out demons."

We know that according to the Bible God's children are the temple of the Spirit of God (see 1 Cor. 3:16). In the Old Testament, the temple had three parts: the holy of holies, the holy place, and the outer court. This picture is a type or representation of who we are as His temple today.

The Shekinah glory of God, or God's "presence," was in the holy of holies. This part of the temple represents our spirits. But when Jesus went into the temple to drive out the thieves and moneychangers, He did not go into the holy of holies. He went into the outer court, where these evildoers were carrying on their business transactions.

The whole account is a picture of deliverance--of what Jesus wants to do in our temples. There may be demonic thieves in our lives that are operating in our outer courts (bodies or souls). Even though they cannot enter the holy of holies (our spirits), Jesus wants them expelled because the temple of God was never intended to be a place for thieves to operate. It is meant to be a place of worship and a place of prayer.

A Covenant Right

Those who believe that the ministry of deliverance is not for believers need to reconsider their position. The truth is, rather, that deliverance is not for the unbeliever. What good would it do to cast demons out of an unbeliever, unless he is planning to get saved?

Unbelievers cannot maintain their deliverance. In fact, according to Luke 11:24-26, after undergoing deliverance, the unsaved person is subject to receiving seven times as many demons as he had before.

The ministry of deliverance is the covenant right of believers. Like every other blessing from God--healing, prosperity, miracles and so on--it is promised only to His covenant people, those who believe in Jesus and come to God through Christ's blood. God, in His mercy, will bless people outside the covenant because He is merciful. But primarily, His blessings are based on covenant. Written by: John Eckhardt

http://www.charismamag.com/spirit/spiritual-growth/846-why-a-christian-can-have-a-demon

*12. Like A Snake in a Gunnysack
(1982)

My wife and I were pastoring a church in Chambersburg, Pennsylvania. The former pastor and his wife had moved to Louisiana and were trusting us to pastor this church which they had begun. There were a lot of problems in his little church, and they had just gone through a major split. I did not want to pastor this church because I saw that there was a lot of head knowledge but no true heart faith. But my wife and I both knew in our hearts that God wanted us to pastor this church.

Within this fellowship, there was a young man by the name of Dwight. I think he was about 22 years old. We took him to our house, letting him sleep in our basement. At the time, we only had our son Michael who was approximately two years old. Dwight had a lot of issues which we were trying to help him deal with. It was evident that there was a lot of deceit and lying going on in his life.

One Sunday morning, one of the brothers, Eric, came to us and informed us that there was a major problem. He told us that his young ten year old daughter had received a letter from Dwight that was rather inappropriate and infringed on the edge of indecent. There was only one elder in the church at the time. I read the letter from Eric and agreed that this letter was not appropriate. At the end of the service, I had my elder meet me in my office with Dwight. I confronted this young man about the letter that he had written to this girl. He openly admitted that he had done it and that it was wrong. He said he desperately wanted prayer to be free from this problem. At the time, I thought it was just a problem he was having with this young girl, but I was completely wrong. When we laid hands on him, the power of God came upon him, and he fell down.

As he was lying on the floor, I heard the Spirit of God very strongly with in my heart say, **"Cast the devils out of him!"** I mean this unction was so strong in my heart that I shook my head a little bit. You see, I had gone to the extreme at one time thinking that every problem in the believer's life was a demon. Now I had swung to the opposite persuasion, thinking that Christians could not have demons. But actually, I discovered that Christians could have demons; just every problem is not a devil. I heard the voice of God once again say, **"Cast the devils out of him!"**

As I looked down at Dwight, I saw something very peculiar and strange. He was a little bit of a heavyset young man, and as I looked at the area of his stomach, it looked to me like there was something turning and twisting in his abdomen. I mean his whole stomach was moving like it was a snake in a gunnysack. I am not exaggerating this in the least. It looked like there was a snake maneuvering in his stomach. I rubbed my eyes, shook my head and told myself that I just imagined it.

Well, to my shame, I completely ignored the voice of God. There was no way that this man had a devil, or so I thought. We left the church that morning with Dwight promising he would never write a letter to this young girl again. He promised that from that moment forward; he would leave her alone. I think it was on Wednesday the same week before I received a phone call from one of the people in the church. They asked me, Pastor, have you picked up the newspaper? I said no, why? They said that Dwight had been arrested! I asked for what? He went down to a local elementary school and was passing notes through the fence to the little girls. I said, no way! Yes, Pastor, they arrested him for offering money to these little girls to do inappropriate things.

At that moment, the Spirit of God strongly reproved me, informing me that this did not have to happen. That if I would have simply obeyed and cast the devils out of Dwight then he would not be in jail at this time. The next Sunday, my elder, came to me telling me that he needed to speak to me. We met in my office, and he told me something incredible. He said Pastor; I need to repent. I asked what for? He said last week when we prayed for Dwight, the Spirit of God told me to cast the devil out of him. I said really? He said yes. And Pastor, did you see what was happening while he was on the floor? I said what do you mean? He said that it looked like there was a snake, a large snake, twisting and turning in his stomach. I had to admit to him that I had seen the same thing, yet had done nothing about it. We both stood there realizing how stupid and disobedient we had been. May God give us a spirit of discernment and a heart of obedience!

*13.Almost Possessed by demons (1976)

Thank God for His wonderful mercy, kindness, and goodness. Even when we fall short, He's still there to help us, protect us and to keep us. There was a brief period in my life after I gave my heart to Christ that I backslid. I was like a yo-yo in my walk with God for maybe two months; messing up, repenting, walking with

God and then messing up again, just to start the cycle over. Everything is a little bit foggy about those particular days. I had come back to Wisconsin from being in Alaska, doing missionary work with the Yupik Indians. Before I left Alaska, depression began to hit me hard. You see, I did not have enough depth in the Word of God. Not only that but I was not attending a good, Spirit-filled Word Church. There was no spirit filled church at that time available in Dillingham, Alaska. (I have heard from some good sources that there is now an Assembly of God church there.) I began to go into deep depression out there on the mud flats of Alaska. Here it was, the middle of winter and 40° below with the wind and the snow whipping around my little wooden shack made from a tent frame. I found myself beginning to dabble back into drugs and alcohol. I knew that I was in big time trouble, so while I still had a little money left, I bought a ticket back to my hometown in Wisconsin.

When I got back to Mukwonago, I began to try to share my faith once again. During this time I was able to land a job in Waukesha, Wisconsin at a company that built transformers for high voltage lines. It was a very good paying job, but I was completely unsatisfied. I could not find any believers. I'm talking about people who were excited about Jesus Christ and who wanted to go all the way. I found myself beginning to visit the bars where I used to hang out. In the beginning, I was simply there to share my faith and drink soda, but before I knew it, I was having a beer here and there. One night, I ran into an old friend who was also driving a motorcycle. I never planned on drinking a lot of beers that night, but I did. Before I knew what I was doing, I was out on this cold, rainy night driving my motorcycle with this old friend. I remember hitting speeds that night of over 100 miles an hour. As I watched the gravel speeding past my front tire, I noticed that sometimes the tire was barely on the asphalt of the road as I'd take the corners at high speeds.

We finally ended up in the community where we both lived. I pulled up to a stop sign, and when I stopped, I fell over onto my right hand side. I was eventually able to pick my 750 Honda up into an upright position; just to have it fall again to my left. I was utterly and completely drunk. How in the world did I just come through the wet, curving, hilly back country roads of Wisconsin? It had to have been God keeping me alive that night. I could not even keep my bike standing up at a stop sign let alone safely ride at speeds of over 100 miles an hour on wet, curving roads! Thank God for His mercy, patience and everlasting kindness! I know that I kept the angels busy that night!

I had begun to backslide. It was a spasmodic, backslidden condition. I would fall into sin, repent and get back up. This continued for a couple of months until one night when I had fallen asleep in an almost drunken condition. While I was asleep, I had this extremely scary and realistic dream. In this dream, it was late at night, and I was just coming out of a bar. I was looking at myself as if I was the third person. I could see that I had been drinking by the way that I was stumbling around, falling and getting back up again. I finally made it to the curb where there was a gutter. I then fell face down, lying in this dirty, filthy, nasty, sewage gutter. People were walking by me and just staring. None were trying to help me out of the sewage in any way whatsoever. Suddenly, as I'm lying in this filthy gutter, I no longer am looking upon myself as a third person. I am in my body when suddenly, demonic forces came flooding into me. I mean demons began to enter into my body, and I began to lose complete control as if I had gone into an epileptic seizure. You cannot believe the absolute horror and fear that filled my heart at that moment.

This experience was so real and frightening to me at the time that I immediately woke up sweating and crying. I fell on my knees next to my bed repenting with everything inside of me for giving place to the devil; for returning to sins that I had come out of in which Christ had delivered me. I knew at that moment that this was a divine warning from God. Scripture says that once a house is clean, the devil will come back to where he had been cast out and if the house where he had been cast out is empty; he will bring back with him seven more spirits worse than himself.

This was the Spirit of God showing me the reality of where I was headed. Right then and there I knew in my heart that I had to leave my hometown. I had to quit my good paying job and run for my life back to God with everything inside of me. Thank God from that time to now I have lived for Christ!

Matthew 12:45Then goeth he, and taketh with himself seven other spirits more wicked than himself, and they enter in and dwell there: and the last state of that man is worse than the first.

*14. Spirit of murder on Herbert (2010)

He Was There To Murder Me & Everyone in Our Church! One day I received a phone call from a gentleman who said he desperately needed help. He was extremely mentally and emotionally tormented by devils. Immediately I perceive there was a spirit of suicide upon him. I prayed with him over the phone, encouraging him to seek the Lord, and to give his heart to Jesus. I told him that any time he needed prayer he could call me. So began a strange relationship with him calling and me praying, and taking authority over the demonic powers that were behind his problems.

Eventually, this particular gentleman showed up at one of our church services. I knew in my heart that there was a heavy spirit of murder on him. I would lay my hands on him praying over him in every service, binding these tormenting and murdering evil spirits that were at work in his life. He began to come to our services on a regular basis. As I was ministering to this particular person, things began to be revealed that were extremely troubling. It turns out that he had been in a mental institution receiving extensive care, even to the point of shock treatments.

The realization of this man being capable of murdering the congregation plus others began to weigh heavily on my heart. One Sunday morning as I came across the parking lot to the church, this man was sitting in his truck just staring straight ahead. I knew immediately he had come there that morning with the intent to murder us all. It was during the time of summer, so his window was rolled down. I walked up to him, as he sat in his truck, looking him directly in the eyes. I told him: Henry (not his real name) you are not going to do it! He said! What? I told him once again: you are not going to do it, in the name of Jesus, do you hear me! He just stared at me, not saying a word. He started his truck up, pulled out of the parking lot, and went down the road.

During a time of counseling, he would tell me that he did not want to hurt his son, his daughter-in-law, or his grandchildren. I told him in the name of Jesus, binding the demonic powers, you will not do this. Now you might ask me, why did you not contact the authorities? I did contact them, informing them what was going on. Unbelievably they told me there was nothing they could do about it until they had proof that he meant us or somebody else harm. In my investigation, I also discovered that he had a permit to carry. I could hardly believe that they would give this mentally unstable man, who had been in a mental institution, given shock treatments a permit to carry!

At this point, I sense in my heart I needed to get a permit to carry a pistol to protect the church members and my family. I also bought a very reliable, and good quality gun. One of the members of our church has a firing range where his son, who is a policeman, and other law officials target practice. As a young man, I had been given training on shooting guns and used to go hunting by myself at the age of 12. I had also spent time in the military, so I was not a complete stranger to firearms. I spent sufficient time shooting at this target range to where I could hit a target pretty accurately with that pistol up to 60 to 80 feet away.

I began to carry this pistol tucked beneath my belt behind my suit jacket whenever I sensed that I needed to take it to church. Sure enough, every time it was quickened in my heart to take the pistol, this gentleman would be at our church. As the months went by, I perceive that he was getting worse. One day in our Sunday morning service we had a special guest speaker who was preaching. This particular gentleman was sitting in the back of the sanctuary.

I had not told anybody about this situation but my wife and my children. Out of the blue, this woman preacher stopped preaching (Jack Coe's daughter) and pointed her finger directly at Henry. She said out loud in front of everybody: I bind that murdering spirit in you. You will not do anyone any harm in Jesus name. People had no idea what she was talking about, but I knew. I was standing in the back of the sanctuary with my pistol tucked behind my suit coat, under my belt. After Joanna had said this, she began to preach once again.

After this incident, I think this gentleman only came back to our church for another month and a half, but then he just simply disappeared. That has probably been about six years ago (2010). I have no idea whatever happened to him. I still continue to pray for him, and for the safety of those he comes in to contact with. We are living in a day and age where we must be extremely sensitive to what God is telling us. Many people are dying because they do not know or are not listening to the voice of God's Holy Spirit. The Lord has rescued my loved ones and me more times than I can tell you because I heard the Lord speaking to my heart.

*15. An Atheist Saved, Healed, Delivered!

Vicki had come to me (being her pastor) with great concern about her sister Connie. Her sister was not only an atheist, but she had begun to dabble into satanic activities, and was now demonized, and was also experiencing great physical afflictions. On numerous occasions, Vicki came to the front of the church after service and I prayed with her about her sister. After one service I perceived in my heart that if God did not divinely intervene in her sister's life in the very near future that not only would Connie lose her soul, but that she was headed for a very tragic death. I encouraged Vicki to go even deeper in prayer for her sister, and that I would join her. Up to this time I had never met Connie, but the Lord had laid her upon my heart in a very real way. The next time Sunday when I saw Vicki, I encouraged her to get her sister to come to one of our services. That I believed if God could get her sister to come up from West Virginia, he would do something amazing for her. Vicki began to strongly encourage her sister to attend one of our services, but she strongly resisted all of Vicki's encouragements.

One Sunday Vicki came to me, informing me that her sister Connie had to be hospitalized for surgery. While she was in the hospital for surgery, she contracted a very deadly infection called MRSA. *MRSA stands for methicillin-resistant Staphylococcus aureus. It is a "staph" germ that does not get better with many of antibiotics that usually cure staph infections. Most staph germs are spread by skin-to-skin contact (touching). A doctor, nurse, other health care provider, or visitors to a hospital may have staph germs on their body that can spread to a patient. Once the staph germ enters the body, it can spread to bones, joints, the blood, or any organ, such as the lungs, heart, or brain. Serious staph infections are more common in people with chronic (long-term) medical problems. Each year, 90,000 Americans suffer from invasive MRSA infection, and about 20,000 die.*

The MRSA was so bad that the doctors had to put a stint in her chest where they could administer antibiotics a couple of times a day directly into her main arteries. When she finally was released from the hospital, a doctor from the CDC would go to her house several times a week. In the midst of all of this terrible situation, the spirit of the Lord was able to move finally upon Connie's heart. She told her sister Vicki that she was going to come to one of our services no matter how difficult it was to have pastor mike pray for her.

Connie drove up from West Virginia to her sister Vicki's house one Sunday morning. That wonderful Sunday morning Vicki, Connie, and her sister Linda, all walked in together as that the service had already begun. God did an amazing miracle in Connie's life that morning. Vicki said: as we walked into the church, GODS presence was so strong that Linda and I started weeping right away. We all three sat down as everyone in the congregation was praying for each other and it looked like everybody was weeping in the service because of the presence of God. The spirit of the Lord was so strong in this service that I do not even remember Pastor Mike preaching. I simply remember everybody praying and worshiping the Lord.

During the service my sister Connie had her eyes closed as she was praying and sincerely crying out to the Lord. The atheism that she had clung to, simply seem to melt off of her as if it had never existed. Connie later informed Linda and me that as she had her eyes closed praying that she had heard a voice say: **Get on Your Knees**. She said in her heart that she could not do this because both of her kneecaps had been replaced with metal. She said the voice said to her again: **Get on Your Knees**.

This voice was so strong within our heart that she decided to do what she had heard no matter what it took. At that very moment, Connie bent her legs and got down on her knees. As she went to her knees Connie said that someone laid hands on her and was praying for her, she thought it was pastor Mike at the time. Vicki, later on, said that she had seen her sister go to her knees, but that no one was there praying for her. We now believe that it was Jesus himself laying his hands upon her sick, fevered, germ infested and broken body. At that very moment, Jesus completely healed Connie from the MRCA. Not only did the Lord deliver her from the staph infection, but healed her knees to where when she walked out of the church she threw away her cane. That morning Connie gave her heart to Jesus and was filled with the Holy Ghost. When Connie later went back to the hospital for bloodwork because of the MRCA, they kept testing her because they could not find the infection. Nine times they tested her for the MRCA but praise the Lord it was gone. The doctors were completely shocked by this discovery!

CHAPTER SIX

How One Becomes Demon Possessed!

There are multiple ways in which demonic entities can find a way into our lives. Becoming demon possessed, or becoming demonized is not usually something that happens instantly. The enemy begins to work in small increments inch by inch into a persons life! We knowingly or unknowingly begin to surrender and yield our wills to him. I guess you could say it is like how someone becomes intoxicated with alcohol. Some begin to drink very slowly and eventually become completely drunk. Others will chug the liquor soul when it hits them it seems to be instantaneous.

Can a person unwittingly, or maybe even unwillingly become demonized? The answer to this question is: **Yes!** Many who are involved in extremely immoral lifestyles were raped, molested and taken advantage of when they were children. The demonic powers that were in operation in those who perform such wicked deeds upon these young people entered in to these poor victims. Because these children did not know how to combat wicked spirits, they unknowingly gave into them.

Through the years of being a pastor, I have dealt with many people who as children were molested or taken advantage of. Many of them are now the victimizers even as they were victimized. The same spirit that was operating in those who victimized them is now operating in them. Can they overcome these demonic powers? Absolutely, but they must give their hearts and lives completely over to Jesus Christ.

As parents, it is our responsibility to protect our children, and yet many parents unknowingly (yes even Christian parents) have opened the door wide to their precious children being demonized. It happens by the entertainment, associations, even by the actions of the parents themselves that are committed. As a young child, I became demonized, suicidal, and destructive because of what was going on in my home. I do not share this story to ridicule or lay blame upon my parents. They did not know better because they had not had a relationship with Jesus Christ.

Am I the devil? (1963)

If my mother was still alive, she could tell you all of the heart aches that I caused her. I do remember as a young child being extremely tormented. I am sure that my parents loved me in whatever capacity they understood. I never heard my dad tell me that he loved me until I was approximately 23 years old. And that was after four years of me telling him every time that I spoke to him that I loved him. That began when I gave my heart to Jesus as a 19-year-old boy. He only once told me that he loved me and yet, to this day, I remember him speaking those words to me over the telephone. Tears rolled down my face when he said that to me.

As a very young child, I remember going out of my way to torment my older brother and sister. I just couldn't help myself. My mother was so exasperated on one occasion that she screamed at me, **"You Are the Devil Himself!"**

Those words were like a dagger to my heart. I do not think that we understand the power of our words. I remember going into our little bathroom in our two-bedroom house. I closed the door and climbed onto the sink where I could see my face in the mirror. Then I took my two little hands and began to rub them over the top of my head and, sure enough, to my shock and my amazement, there were two lumps on my head. I could feel a lump on my left side and a lump on my right side. I was the devil! And the horns were beginning to form on my head. I remember to this day weeping, knowing that I had no hope of salvation because I was the devil himself!

Matthew 15:22 And, behold, a woman of Canaan came out of the same coasts, and cried unto him, saying, Have mercy on me, O Lord, thou son of David; my daughter is grievously vexed with a devil.

Choking Cuddles & Peanuts

When a person who is tormented, of course, they will torment others. We can only reproduce from what we are or take people to where we live. If you are miserable and tormented, full of sin and wickedness, that's all you can produce. My parents used to have beagles as their number one choice of dogs. We would go rabbit hunting with them whenever the opportunity arose. I did eventually purchase a Redbone Coon hound puppy which I raised to hunt raccoons.

My mom had two small beagles which she kept in the house. Their names were Cuddles and Peanuts. I don't think my parents ever really understood how tormented I was. My heart and mind even as a young boy was twisted and sick. When no one else was around, I would call these two little beagles to me taking them one at a time. (I truly do not even want to share these stories, but I believe they will show you that there is hope for anyone and everyone.) I would take Cuddles into my lap, petting and cuddle her, and then I would put my hands on her throat and begin to choke her. Yes, I would begin to choke her with everything inside of me. I would choke poor little Cuddles until her tongue would hang out of her mouth until it seemed like there was no life left in her. Until her body went completely limp.

And then, when it would seem like she was almost dead, I would stop choking her. And then I would begin to cry and weep, begging her not to die, asking God to let her live. I would be shaking her trying to get her to breathe again. And, sure enough, she would begin to breathe and come back around. When she was completely recovered and was breathing normally again, I would start it all over. Yes, you heard correctly. My sick, tormented nature would grab her by the throat again, and I would repeat the cycle. Once again I would begin to cry, asking her to live. And then I would start it all over again.

I not only did this to our dog Cuddles but also Peanut. I never did it where anybody could see me. Neither my mother, father, brother or sister ever suspected what I was doing. I was one little sick, tormented boy. These actions only reconfirmed to me that I was the Devil himself in human flesh.

Luke 9:42 And as he was yet a coming, the devil threw him down, and tare him. And Jesus rebuked the unclean spirit, and healed the child, and delivered him again to his father.

I Joined the Navy in 1973

To this day it amazes me that the government accepted me into the Navy back in 1973 when I was 17 years old. At the time I had major mental, emotional and even physical problems which included hearing problems and a major speech impediment. I quit school at 15 years old, leaving home until I ended up in trouble with the law at 16. I was very suicidal from the age of 16 until I was 19 years old. Waves of depression would overwhelm me. Of upon myself at times driving my car on the opposite side of the road headed for the vehicles in front of me. On numerous occasions, it was an absolute miracle that I did not have a head-on collision with the cars I was headed for. When I ended up in trouble with the law, I was given the option of joining the military are being persecuted. *prosecuTed*.

I chose the military. However, for the military to accept me, I had to have my GED. Subsequently, I worked extremely hard to get it, and I succeeded. At the time, I believed that joining the Navy would take me out of the drugs, violence, immorality and alcohol lifestyle that I had been living. That could not have been farther from the truth. As soon as I graduated from basic training, Uncle Sam shipped me to San Diego, California for further training on repairing 16mm projectors. Upon accomplishing this training, I was sent to Adak, Alaska in the Aleutian Islands. I was assigned to the special services department. They provided all of the entertainment for the men on base. This included the movie theater, bowling alley, a roller-skating rink, horse stables for taking men hunting and the cafeteria (not the chow hall).

I was extremely unreliable and incompetent, so much so that within the two years that I was there, I was transferred to every one of those facilities. My last job ended up being at the horse stables shoveling manure. During this time I was heavily involved in drugs, including selling them. I was drinking a lot of alcohol including ripple wine, vodka, and tequila. I smoked an average of 3 1/2 packs of cigarettes per day, not including cigars. I used Brown Mule, Copenhagen, Beach Nut, and Skoal chewing tobaccos. My favorite singing groups were Dr. Hook and the Medicine Band, Pink Floyd, The Grateful Dead and America.

When I was off duty, my attire was extremely strange. First off, when I was younger, my older brother knocked out my front tooth. Of course, I had it replaced with a pegged tooth, but while I was stationed in Adak, it got knocked out again. As a result, I picked up a ridiculous nickname. I was called "Tooth." I wanted to fit in with the cowboy crowd, so I found an old cowboy hat which was way too large for me. To make it fit, I took an old military ski hat and sewed it on the inside so that it would be snug on my head. (Of course, this old Stetson cowboy hat was way too large for me.) As I would walk around the base with this large cowboy hat, it would be flopping on top of my head, making me look extremely silly; especially with me missing one of my front teeth.

One day, as I was going to the cafeteria, I happened to spit tobacco on the sidewalk. A young ensign saw me do this, and he made me stop and wipe it up. From then on I decided that I would no longer get in trouble for this, so I picked up the habit of spitting the tobacco juice in my left, front pocket. Why? Because I thought I was cool having the tobacco juices overflowing my pocket. Oh, how the foolish and the degenerate wallow in their mire!

I did not want just to be a cowboy because I was also a hippie. So, with a bright new idea, I went to the cafeteria and asked for all of their chicken necks. I took these chicken necks and boiled them in a pot of hot vinegar water. Then I took these chicken bones after they were cleaned and strung them on a leather strand. I would wear these chicken bones as a necklace around my neck. It stank! No wonder I was extremely depressed all of the time.

*16. GOD SET ME FREE FROM THE DEVIL

I think that you can begin to see what kind of a mess I was. **However, supernaturally one night, God stepped into my life, instantly and radically changing me forever!** My last three months of military life was so amazingly transformed that I was put in charge of working parties and details from time to time. God instantly delivered me from all of my devices including all of my foolish behaviors. I was a new creature in Christ! Christ had supernaturally set me free from the tormenting demonic powers that had possessed my life for so long!

Here is what happened! On my 19th birthday, I was overwhelmed with a demonic spirit of self-pity and depression. I decided to end it all by slitting my wrist! I went into the bathroom with a large, survival hunting knife. I put the knife to my wrist with full intentions of slitting my artery. I was determined to kill myself. I held the knife firmly against my wrist and took one more last breath before I slid it across my wrist. All of a sudden, invisible presence came rushing down upon me like a blanket. It was a tangible, overwhelming presence of mind-boggling fear. It was the fear of God, and it overwhelmed me! Instantly, I realized with the crystal-clear understanding that I was going to hell. I deserved hell; I belonged in hell, and hell had a right to me. Furthermore, I knew if I slit my wrist, I would be in hell forever.

Overwhelming Love

I walked out of that little military bathroom to my bunk. I fell on my knees, reached my hands up toward heaven and cried out to Jesus with all of my heart. All of this was supernatural and strange. I did not ever recall any time when anyone ever shared with me how to become a Christian or how to be converted. I knew how to pray. I cried out to Jesus and told Him I believed He was the Son of God, had been raised from the dead, and I desperately needed Him. I not only asked Him into my heart but I gave Him my heart, soul, mind, and life. At that very instant, a love beyond description came rushing into my heart. I knew what love was for the first time in my life. At the same time, I comprehended what I was placed on this earth for—I was here to follow, love, serve, and obey God. A deep love and hunger to know God grabbed my heart. I was filled with love from top to bottom, inside and out—inexpressibly beyond belief. Jesus had come to live inside of me!

Instantaneous Deliverance

I was instantly delivered: from over three packs of cigarettes a day, from worldly and satanic music, from chewing tobacco; from cussing and swearing, from drugs and alcohol, and from a filthy and dirty mind.

Some might ask why my conversion was so dramatic. I believe that it's because I had nothing to lose. I knew down deep that there was not one single thing worth saving in me. The only natural talent I ever possessed was the ability to mess things up. At the moment of salvation, I completely surrendered my heart and life to Jesus Christ.

Dr Michael H Yeager

I BECAME HUNGER FOR GOD'S WORD!

I remember after giving my heart to Jesus Christ that I got up from the floor born again, saved and delivered, I was a brand-new person. Immediately hunger and thirst for the Word of God took a hold of me. I began to devour Matthew, Mark, Luke, and John. I just could not get enough of the word of God because of my love for Jesus Christ and his Father. Jesus became my hero in every area of my thoughts and daily life. He became my reason for getting up and going to work, eating, sleeping, and living. I discovered that everything I did was based on the desire of wanting to please Him. I carried my little green military Bible with me wherever I went.

Whenever I had an opportunity, I would open it up and study it. It wasn't very long before I believed for a larger Bible. This larger Bible gave me much more room to make notes, highlight and circle certain Scriptures. The more I fed on the Scriptures, the greater my hunger became for them. I probably was not saved even for two months when I was asked to speak for the 1st time at a small Pentecostal church. I believe it was called Adak Full Gospel Church. As far as I know, it was the only Pentecostal church on this military base situated on an Aleutian Island in Alaska. Since 1975 I have never lost my hunger or my thirst for God's word. I can truly say even what the psalmist said!

Psalm 104:34 My meditation of him shall be sweet: I will be glad in the Lord.

This hunger for God's word has caused me to memorize over a 3rd of the New Testament. I am not bragging or boasting; I'm just simply saying that God's word is the joy and rejoicing of my heart. There are People Who Love to Swim, People Who Love to Work out, People Who Love to Do Push-Ups and Chin-Ups and Lift Weights, but we need people who love God's word!

God Healed Me of Being Tongue-Tied!

After I had given my heart to Christ, a divine hunger and thirst for the Word of God began to possess me. I practically devoured Matthew, Mark, Luke, and John. Jesus became my hero in every sense of the word, in every area of my thoughts and daily living. He became my soul reason for getting up every day and going to work, eating, sleeping, and living. I discovered that everything I did was based on a desire of wanting to please Him.

One day I was reading my Bible and discovered where Jesus said that it was necessary for him to leave. That because when he would go back to the Father, he would send the promise of the Holy Ghost to make us a witness. Furthermore, I learned it was His will for me to be filled to overflowing with the Holy Ghost and that the Holy Ghost would empower and equip me to be a witness an ambassador for God. The Holy Ghost would also lead me and guide me into all truth.

With all of my heart, I desperately wanted to reach the lost for Jesus Christ for they could experience the same love and freedom that I was now walking in. I searched the Scriptures to confirm this experience. In the book of Joel, in the old covenant, the four Gospels and especially in the book of acts I discovered the will of God when it comes to this baptism. I perceived in my heart that I needed to receive this baptism the same way that I had received salvation. I had to look to Christ and trust by faith that he would give to me this baptism of the Spirit. It declared in the book of acts that after they had been baptized in the Holy Ghost, they all began to speak in a heavenly language. I had not been around what we would call Pentecostal people, so I had never heard anybody else speak in this heavenly language. But that did not matter to me because it was within the Scriptures.

Acts 2:39 For the promise is unto you, and to your children, and to all that are afar off, even as many as the Lord our God shall call.

I remember getting on my knees next to my bunk bed where I cried out and asked God to fill me with the Holy Ghost so I could be a witness. As I was crying out to God, something began to happen on the inside of me. It felt like hot buckets of oil was beginning to be poured upon me and within me. Something then began to rise out of my innermost being. Before I knew what I was doing, a new language came out bubbling of my mouth which I had never heard before, or been taught to speak. I began to speak in a heavenly tongue.

Now up to this time I had a terrible speech impediment. You see I had been born tongue-tied. Yes they had operated on me, and I had gone to speech therapy, and yet most people could not understand what I was saying. I could not even pronounce my last name YEAGER properly. My tongue simply refused to move in a way in which I could pronounce my Rs.

After I was done praying in this new language, I discovered to my absolute surprise that my speech impediment was instantly and completely gone! From that time on, I have never stopped preaching Jesus Christ. For almost 40 years I have proclaimed the truth of Jesus Christ to as many as I can.

For the First Time She Could Understand Me

About four months after I gave my heart to Christ I went back to my hometown, Mukwonago, Wisconsin, and I immediately went to see one of my best friends to share with him my conversion experience. Actually, it was his sister I had been dating for the last three years. I wrote her a letter telling her what happened to me, and how God gloriously had set me free from drugs, alcohol, and all of my worldly living. This caused her to cut me off completely as if I had lost my mind. Praise God! I had lost my mind by receiving the mind of Christ. My friend's mother was listening while I was speaking to her son, and out of nowhere she said, "Mike, what happened to you?" I told her how I had been delivered from drugs and immorality because I gave my heart to Jesus. She said, "No, that's not what I'm talking about. After many years of knowing you, this is the 1st time I can fully understand what you are saying."

You see, my speech was so garbled that it was very difficult for people to understand truly exactly what I was saying. Those who know me now would not have recognized the old me. Before I got baptized in the Holy Ghost, you would not have been able to understand most of I said. I'm still trying to make up for the 1st nineteen years when I could not speak properly.

2 Corinthians 5:17 Therefore if any man be in Christ, he is a new creature: old things are passed away; behold, all things are become new.

How One Young Lady Became Demonized!

I grew up in the countryside in a seemingly happy family. When I was 13 years old, we moved into town and from then on my life went downhill. I made a new group of friends, and together we tried out everything we wanted to do. In the beginning, we started with stealing Dad's beer and getting drunk in the park, but soon we started doing séances (talking to spirits through an Ouija-board) at birthday parties. At first, we thought one of us was playing tricks on the others, only to finally realize that no one was; there was a spiritual realm! During these times we started to smoke marijuana and hang out with boys who were much older than us.

This spiritual realm enticed me, so I looked deeper into it, and watched demonic movies about people being possessed. I wanted to do séances' by myself, and I knew that all I had to do was to invite a spirit. Knowing that this was unsafe, I still went ahead and did it. From this time on I developed into a binge-drinker and "regular-smoker", spending more time attending parties and drinking sessions than going to school. The group of friends I hung around with would always smoke marijuana at school. Naturally, my grades quickly dropped from A's to D's, and soon I was the teachers' nightmare student. I became an outcast at school. By year 10 I wasn't learning properly because of my wild ways. Changing schools did not help, and I failed at my new school, too. My family life was shocking. I was loved so much by my parents, but I abused them. At home my sister and I argued with each other and with our parents; by the age of 15 my younger sister had moved out, and I moved out when I was 16.

Having moved out, it didn't take long, and I started injecting too and then I moved in with my boyfriend. At the time I didn't realize that I was living in a house full of drug addicts, but within a few months I had tried taking amphetamines; I saw my friend injecting, and of course, having the attitude that I could do anything, I did too. I stayed awake for three days. Life seemed great, even though through sober eyes we were living in squalor.

At 17, I left town to go travelling around Australia. For three years I continued to take drugs, drink, meet strange men, and party. At this time my life hit an all-time low, and it was during this period that I made a new friend whom I travelled with for some time. We took drugs and partied together. After a holiday, she came back and told me that she had been baptized as a Christian. I took no notice and continued in my filthy ways.

In February 2007, I was working in Melbourne and spending my weekends clubbing and taking drugs. One morning we met some people who gave us free drugs. I didn't want them but gave in to the temptation. We stayed up all night. By morning I had severe paranoia. This was common for me when I got high on "speed", but never with such intensity. I told my friend that I was scared, but I didn't know what of. I went into the bathroom. Looking in the bathroom mirror, I didn't recognize myself. I told myself that I needed help, not knowing what was wrong, or who to get help from.

I left the house trying to escape, and as I began to think back through recent events, I knew that I was demonically possessed.

After a while, I rang my friend who had recently become a Christian. I told her about these manifestations, not knowing if she would believe me or not. My friend phoned for help and was able to speak with a Christian friend, who gave her advice. She the read scriptures from the Bible to me.

MATTHEW 4:23-24 "And Jesus went about all Galilee, teaching in their synagogues, and preaching the gospel of the kingdom, and healing all manner of sickness and all manner of disease among the people. And his fame went throughout all Syria: and they brought unto him all sick people that were taken with divers diseases and torments, and those which were possessed with devils, and those which were lunatic, and those that had the palsy; and he healed them."

Possessed by now, I knew I needed help At that point I realized that if there is a devil, there has to be a God. I concluded that only Jesus could free me from this evil spirit, and I needed His help.

The next day, Monday, I wanted to go downtown and look for a church that could help me. My friend wanted to come with me to make sure I was safe, but I didn't want her to see me like this. So I went alone, thinking that I could contain the spirit. To my horror, I couldn't, and as I walked down the street I started growling and screaming. I tried to hide my face, but onlookers saw this young girl screaming as she hurried down the street. I found a church which was locked, which made me howl even more. I found another, but that was closed too. I went to the little house beside the church and asked for the pastor. Each time I looked at the cross I screamed so loudly. I sat down with the man, told him my story, and tried to read the Bible. It was hard to concentrate, and the spirit wasn't giving up so easily.

Realizing there was nothing they could do I continued screaming and howling so loudly that people on the street could hear me. Two counsellors walking past heard me and came to try and help. Realizing there was nothing they could do, they called nurses, who called an ambulance. There was no way I was going to a hospital! The police were also called, but I wouldn't budge. I had grabbed hold of a fence and wouldn't let go. I told them to ring my friend, and she came to the scene. Together we got into the ambulance and drove off with the sirens blaring. I knew what kind of help I needed and that I wasn't going to get it from them.

I was taken to a psychiatric hospital and locked in a cell alone. Nurses and doctors looked at me through the window. It took six nurses to inject me with a sedative while I screamed in objection. I pleaded with them not to give me drugs, and eventually I collapsed in exhaustion. For four days I was locked up in the hospital. My friend came and saw me every day. She told me the only way I would ever get out would be to pretend nothing was wrong. I was able to suppress the spirit for a while, and the doctor labelled me as suffering from a drug-induced psychosis, but I knew that I was possessed.

I was released from the hospital, and for another two months I held down a job and hoped the spirit would go away. I went to a Catholic church to get the spirit exorcised from me, but all they did was put oil on my head and say a prayer for me. I knew I was still possessed, and that the priest had got it wrong. One afternoon my friend and I had an argument which led her to leave work early, and I walked home a few hours later. I could feel this thing in my throat. I dropped my head back and screamed as I walked down the highway. I got home and threw myself down on the grass, screaming in pain. I knew that I had to get rid of this thing, so we packed up soon after I got home and left town. We drove right through the state, heading for Coffs Harbour, and made it within a few days.

There I met some Christians who had helped my friend, and they talked to me about the **Word of God**. I knew that only Jesus could save me, and I sincerely wanted Him to. I was prepared to give up my life for Him if He would set me free from this evil spirit. As they preached, my head dropped back, and I fell into another fit. After many scriptures and questions I couldn't bear the pain anymore, and just wanted to be baptized and receive the gift of the Holy Spirit as the Bible says in:

ACTS 2:38 "...Repent, and be baptized every one of you in the name of Jesus Christ for the remission of sins, and ye shall receive the gift of the Holy Ghost."

We headed for the beach where I was baptized by full immersion. I pictured myself being filled with light as I was prayed over and I received the Holy Spirit instantly while still in the water. **I realized that I was no longer possessed by this evil spirit, but filled with the amazing Spirit of God. I was instantly set free from the bondage and pain. All I could do was smile and praise God for His gift of salvation.**

I still thank Him and praise Him for His power over Satan which has set me free. He completely forgave my sinful life, and I have never had any withdrawal symptoms from drugs and am now a new creature in Christ. "Therefore if any man is in Christ, he is a new creature: old things are passed away; behold, all things become new." (2 CORINTHIANS 5:17). Since I have chosen to follow God, He has taught me how to live a clean life. He completely forgave my sinful life, which is why Jesus died.

"But God commendeth his love toward us, in that, while we were yet sinners, Christ died for us." (ROMANS 5:8)

*17. Committing Suicide: Then God Showed up
(1994)

God is wanting to lead and guides us with peace and joy. This is a divine inner manifestation of God's presence. It is not based on your feelings, circumstances, or situation. I had a very close and good friend of mine (Dale) who shared with me how he first experiences this amazing peace and joy. He told me that he was all wrapped up in drugs, alcohol, immorality and wild living. One night he had just come home from a wild night on the town, and he was standing on the deck of his back porch at 11 in the morning extremely depressed and hopeless. He stood on the outside deck contemplating suicide because he was so stinking miserable. He hated his life and everything about it.

As he was standing there, he finally cried out to God from his heart, surrendering his life to Jesus Christ. As he gave his heart to Jesus, something wonderful and amazing happened. It seemed like all of nature was singing at once he told me! As he looked out over the valley behind his house, and it was like all of nature was singing to him. The peace of God overwhelmed him from head to toe, even to the ends of his fingertips he told me. The sky was bluer then he had ever seen it. The grass was greener, the trees were greener and more full of life, the flowers were more beautiful and brilliant than he had ever seen them. Christ had come into his heart and completely changed every perception that he had ever had.

One minute he was so tormented that he wanted to end his miserable life, and the next minute he was so full of life, love, joy and peace that he felt like he had died and gone to heaven. This is the wonderful and marvelous experience of the new birth. When you totally surrender your heart, your mind and your life to Jesus Christ, he comes rushing in like a mighty wind.

He did not realize it at the time, but this was the peace that passes all understanding, the peace that makes you feel like everything is going to be all right no matter what is happening.

CHAPTER SEVEN

HOW PEOPLE ARE DELIVERED!

First What You <u>Do Not Need</u> To Cast Out Devils!

The Holy Cross! Holy Water! The Physical Bible held up in front of the Possessed! Rosary Beads! A Purple Stole - (The stole is a garment that is draped across the shoulders. It's a long scarf that is often decorated with some religious iconography!) Beeswax Candles! A Book of Exorcism Rites - The contents of these books can range from Catholic-specific rituals to Orthodox exorcism prayers to non-denominational prayers of Deliverance! The Blessed Sacrament - (by Performing the sacrament, wafer, wine and all)! Blessed Salt! More than One Person Present! Special Anointed prayers, blessings, or invocations! Ordained Priest, or Ministers (or higher prelate)! Ropes or instruments (people) needed to restrain the demonized! Certain prayers like the Our Father, Hail Mary, or the Athanasian Creeds! You do not need to Plead the Blood! You do not have to be Yelling or Screaming at the demonic powers! A Group of people all praying and commanding evil spirits at the same time to come out! You do not have to ask or get the names of the spirits! You do not need to take days, weeks, or months of constant prayer and exorcisms!

WHAT DO WE NEED?

#1 Christ Must be ~~Exalt~~ *exalted* Above ALL in Your Heart!

Christ was the perfect will of the heavenly Father, manifested and revealed to us in his earthly ministry. We must now learn to exalt Jesus Christ above all and over all the afflictions and attacks of the enemy.

Jesus has ALL Authority and Power in Heaven and Earth!

Matthew 28:18 And Jesus came and spake unto them, saying, All power is given unto me in heaven and in earth.

Colossians 2:15 And having spoiled principalities and powers, he made a shew of them openly, triumphing over them in it.

For this particular truth I will be using **Hebrews chapter 1**, and the gospel of **John chapter 1**. These two chapters will help build an amazing foundation for spiritual discernment, casting out devils in every situation. If you embrace what is revealed in these two chapters, your ability to cast out, devils will be greatly increased. Let us now take a look at Hebrews chapter 1.

Hebrews 1:1 God, who at sundry times and in divers manners spake in time past unto the fathers by the prophets, 2 hath in these last days spoken unto us by his Son, whom he hath appointed heir of all things, by whom also he made the worlds; 3 who being the brightness of his glory, and the express image of his person, and upholding all things by the word of his power, when he had by himself purged our sins, sat down on the right hand of the Majesty on high;

In Hebrews 1 it is revealed that God had spoken to the

fathers by the prophets, but has now spoken to us by his Son Jesus Christ. According to **Ephesians 2:20 the kingdom of God is built upon the apostles and prophets, Jesus Christ himself being the chief cornerstone.** Please notice that in times past God spoke specifically by the prophets to the father's, now we have a surer word of prophecy, a deeper revelation, a more precise understanding of the perfect will of our heavenly Father.

Why? Because he's going to speak to us in a very clear and dramatic way. If we believe the words, the life, and the example of Jesus Christ, it will radically transform our lives and the level of **Divine Authority** that we walk in. Remember all the words and deeds that had been spoken and revealed up to the time of Christ was to prepare us for the **coming of Christ**. The life of Jesus is the perfect will of God manifested in human flesh. This is the mystery which had been hidden before the foundation of the world.

Notice Hebrews 1: in verse 2 *hath in these last days spoken unto us by his Son!* The foundation of my understanding of the will of God, the purposes of God, the plan of God, the mission of God, the mysteries of God, cannot be discovered in any greater revelation than the person of Jesus Christ! **There is no greater revelation of God's perfect divine will or his voice then that which we discover in Jesus Christ.** I cannot emphasize this enough!

If you do not understand that God has revealed himself to us very precisely through his son Jesus Christ, you will end up being mixed up, confused, and led astray. Learning the will of God very precisely is only found in **Jesus Christ**, whom he has appointed heir of all things, by whom also he made the worlds. Notice Hebrews chapter 1:3 boldly declares that Jesus Christ is the brightness of the Father's glory, the manifestation of the Father's presence, and the express image of His personality. Jesus is like a mirror reflecting the perfect image of the heavenly Father to all of humanity. Jesus declared:

John 14:9 Jesus saith unto him, have I been so long time with you, and yet hast thou not known me, Philip? He that hath seen me hath seen the Father; and how sayest thou then, Shew us the Father? 10 Believest thou not that I am in the Father, and the Father in me? The words that I speak unto you I speak not of myself: but the Father that dwelleth in me, he doeth the works.

Jesus Christ is the **absolute perfect will** of the Father revealed to you and me, especially when it comes to healing. The deepest revelation of the Father is only discovered in Jesus Christ! Paul, the apostle, commands us to have the mind of Christ.

Philippians 2:5 Let this mind be in you, which was also in Christ Jesus: 6 who, being in the form of God, thought it not robbery to be equal with God: 7 but made himself of no reputation, and took upon him the form of a servant, and was made in the likeness of men: 8 and being found in fashion as a man, he humbled himself, and became obedient unto death, even the death of the cross.

When we look at Jesus and hear His words, see his works, it is the Father that we are experiencing! The apostle John boldly declares this in John 1.

John 1:1 In the beginning was the Word, and the Word was with God, and the Word was God. 2 The same was in the beginning with God. 3 All things were made by him; and without him was not anything made that was made.

All things were made by the word. What word is it speaking about in these scriptures? Is it talking about the written word or Christ the word? It is obvious that it is talking about the person of Christ Jesus, Emmanuel God with us!

John 1:14 And the Word was made flesh, and dwelt among us, (and we beheld his glory, the glory as of the only begotten of the Father,) full of grace and truth.

The reality is that we have to know the person of Christ

discovered in the four Gospels for us to rightly discern the Word of God. What do I mean by this statement? When I gave my heart to Jesus Christ on February 18, 1975, at about 3 p.m., all I had available was a little military green Bible. At the moment Christ came into my heart, I picked up that little Bible and began to devour it. Matthew, Mark, Luke, and John, the 4 Gospels of Jesus Christ became my favorite books. I just could not get enough of the wonderful reality of Jesus. As I read these 4 Gospels, I walked with Christ every step of the way. From his birth, through his childhood, his baptism by John when he was 30 years old. When he was baptized by the Holy Ghost, and he was led of the Spirit into the wilderness, tempted of the enemy and overcame him by boldly declaring **"It is written."**

I spent my first three years as a believer eating and drinking nothing but Jesus from the four Gospels. Yes, I did read the epistles, and they were wonderful, but nothing captured and captivated my heart as much as the life, the words, and the ministry of Jesus Christ. I wept as I read of his sufferings, his crucifixion, and his death. I wept when I saw that the Heavenly Father had to turn his face away from his own Son for our salvation. **I shouted at the triumphant conquest and victory that Jesus had over every satanic power.**

Jesus Christ is the perfect reflection of the Heavenly Father. There is no more perfect revelation of the will of the Father than Jesus Christ. Actually, I am extremely happy that I was not influenced by the modern day church for the first three years of my salvation. When I eventually came to the lower 48, after living and ministering in Alaska, I was shocked and surprised at what most Christians believed. I did not realize that there was such a large variety of different interpretations of the Scriptures in the church. Many of God's people are extremely confused, sick, and defeated because of a lack of understanding the will of the Father revealed to us in the life, the ministry, the words of Jesus Christ. Many ministers declare insane false doctrines that are so contrary to what I discovered in Christ; it is hard for me to believe that people can even believe what these men are teaching is truth. To truly know the will of God, all you have to do is look at Jesus Christ: His words, deeds, actions, and reactions; His lifestyle and his attitude, mannerism, wonderful character, and the fruit of his life. I can truly say that since I have been born again, I have only had one person who I truly want to be like: **His name is Jesus Christ**.

If the body of Christ would simply go back to the four Gospels, and walk with Jesus every step of the way, from his birth to his resurrection, to his ascension, much of the confusion would be gone when comes to the will of God. I believe the reason why so many believers are being deceived by false doctrines and philosophies, why they are not receiving their deliverance is because they do not know, or understand Jesus Christ.

Hebrews 13:8, "Jesus Christ the same yesterday, and today, and forever."

In the old covenant, God says **"I am the Lord, and I change not."** Without truly seeing the Father by the words of Jesus Christ, and by the life of Jesus Christ you can easily be led astray by crafty men misusing Scriptures. You have to see Jesus to understand not just the Old Testament but also the epistles of the New Testament. Jesus is the voice of God, the absolute perfect will of the Father, the manifestation of God in the earth.

I have heard ministers use the Bible to contradict the teachings of Jesus Christ. The reason why false doctrines have been able to take root in the church is because people have not looked and listened to Jesus in the four Gospels. If in your mind and heart you will exalt Christ and his teaching above all else, it will be very difficult for the enemy to lead you astray with false teachings and doctrines.

Matthew 9:33 And when the devil was cast out, the dumb spake: and the multitudes marvelled, saying, It was never so seen in Israel.

Matthew 10:1 And when he had called unto him his twelve disciples, he gave them power against unclean spirits, to cast them out, and to heal all manner of sickness and all manner of disease.

Matthew 10:8 Heal the sick, cleanse the lepers, raise the dead, cast out devils: freely ye have received, freely give.

Matthew 12:28 But if I cast out devils by the Spirit of God, then the kingdom of God is come unto you.

Mark 16:17 And these signs shall follow them that believe; In my name shall they cast out devils; they shall speak with new tongues;

Luke 11:20 But if I with the finger of God cast out devils, no doubt the kingdom of God is come upon you.

Luke 10:19 Behold, I give unto you power to tread on serpents and scorpions, and over all the power of the enemy: and nothing shall by any means hurt you.

Luke 9:42 And as he was yet a coming, the devil threw him down, and tare him. And Jesus rebuked the unclean spirit, and healed the child, and delivered him again to his father.

Luke 4:36 And they were all amazed, and spake among themselves, saying, What a word is this! for with authority and power he commandeth the unclean spirits, and they come out.

Luke 6:18 And they that were vexed with unclean spirits: and they were healed.

#2 Operate in the Realm of Faith!

The second principle or step in Casting OUT Devils is that you must get into the realm of faith. Jesus taught more on the subject of faith (in the four Gospels) than any other subject. This place, this dimension, this world that we call **FAITH**, is beyond the human equation, or understanding. This goes way beyond the intellect, your feelings, your emotions, and the circumstances of life. Isaiah chapter 55 he says:

Isaiah 55:8 For my thoughts are not your thoughts, neither are your ways my ways, saith the Lord. 9 For as the heavens are higher than the earth, so are my ways higher than your ways, and my thoughts than your thoughts.

In order to get into this reality of **Faith**, it must be accomplished by way of the word of God. The Bible says that natural men did not dream up this book, **the Bible**, but spoke, and wrote as God moved upon them.

2 Peter 1:21 For the prophecy came not in old time by the will of man: but holy men of God spake as they were moved by the Holy Ghost.

We can look at Hebrews chapter 11, where we see amazing miracles, signs, and wonders all accomplished by faith, by men and women just like you and I. In the New Testament, and in the Old Testament, all the way to the end of the Bible, people lived and moved by faith. The only way to get into this world, this realm, this place of **Faith,** were all things are possible, is by unwavering trust and confidence in God, and His Word. Everything that I will share with you in this book is to help bring you into this place called **Faith.** Without faith, it is impossible to please God.

*Hebrews 11:6 But without faith, it is impossible to please him: for he that cometh to God must believe that he is and that he is a rewarder of them that diligently seek him.

Faith is like a diamond with many facets, and yet it is the same diamond!

Faith is spoken of in a very strong way (believe, trust,) over 800 times in the Bible. **Jesus** did more teaching on the subject of faith than anything other subject. I cannot over emphasize the importance of having faith in Christ to Operate in Authority and power!. Before we can go any further, I need to explain what I mean when I say faith. As I read the word of God I discover there is *only one true faith*, that is faith in **CHRIST JESUS!** All other faiths and beliefs, no matter what you may call them, according to the word of God, they are not faith at all! It may be a belief system, a psychological philosophy, but it is not faith.

When Christ ascended up on high, he gave gifts unto men. He gave some apostles, some prophets, some evangelist, pastors and teachers. Now these men and women need to be walking in the **Realm of Faith**. If they are not walking in faith, they cannot bring you into faith. IF they are not walking in **obedience**, they cannot bring you into a place of **obedience**. If they are not walking in deliverance, and freedom, they cannot bring you into that place.

Now, if we as ministers are not submitted to Christ, how can we bring you into that realm of **Submission**? These fivefold ministry gifts that Christ gave should be, and need to be walking in this realm of faith. I'm not discrediting these men and women if they are not walking there, but it will be very difficult for these ministry gifts to help you receive what God has for you if they are not walking in it themselves. Basically, we take people to the place where we are at.

Hebrew 11 gives to us a description of faith and its manifestations. Let's look very briefly at Hebrews 11: 1to 3

Hebrews 11:1-3 Now faith is the substance of things hoped for, the evidence of things not seen. ² For by it the elders obtained a good report. ³ Through faith, we understand that the worlds were framed by the word of God so that things which are seen were not made of things which do appear.

So we can boldly declare that faith is a substance --- that gives evidence -- by which the worlds were framed by the word of God. Only the Christian faith (faith in **CHRIST JESUS**) is what brought about, and continues to sustain creation, and all that exist. It is very important for us to understand that there is **only one faith**! This faith is the **only faith** that saves, heals, delivers, creates, pleases God, and makes all things possible!

Ephesians 4:4-6 There is one body, and one Spirit, even as ye are called in one hope of your calling; ⁵ one Lord, one faith, one baptism, ⁶ one God and Father of all, who is above all, and through all, and in you all.

Did you hear that? There is only **one true faith**, and that is faith in **CHRIST JESUS**! There is no other name under heaven given among men whereby we must be saved, healed, delivered, set free, and transformed! **TRUE FAITH** always takes dominion over the world, the flesh, and the devil! Faith in **Christ** always produces positive results and brings victory in every situation. Many people are operating in presumption, natural reasoning, mental acknowledgment, truly thinking that they are operating in faith (In **Christ Jesus**) when the truth of the matter is --- **they are not!**

1 John 5:3-5 For this is the love of God, that we keep his commandments: and his commandments are not grievous. ⁴ For whatsoever is born of God overcometh the world: and this is the victory that overcometh the world, even our faith. ⁵ Who is he that overcometh the world, but he that believeth that Jesus is the Son of God?

Every human being, when they were conceived within their mother's womb, was invested with the divine seed of faith. It is extremely important that **we acknowledge this reality** so that we do not allow our enemy (the devil) into deceiving us into believing that we have no faith. Not only were we created with faith, but we were created by faith, by **Christ Jesus, God the Father, and the Holy Ghost!**

John 1:3 *All things were made by him, and without him was not anything made that was made.*

Let's take a look at two scriptures discovered in Genesis! Genesis 1:26

And God said, Let us make man in our image, after our likeness: and let them have dominion over the fish of the sea, and over the fowl of the air, and over the cattle, and over all the earth, and over every creeping thing that creepeth upon the earth. :27 So God created man in his own image, in the image of God created he him; male and female created he them.

Did you notice that man was created in the image of God! How does God operate and function? We could talk about the character of God dealing with his love, mercy, forgiveness, long- suffering, gentleness, kindness, meekness, holiness, faithfulness, joy, goodness, and many other attributes, but all of these springs from the fact that he operates in faith. There is a very interesting Scripture that declares this found in the book of Timothy.

2 Timothy 2:13 If we believe not, yet he abideth faithful: he cannot deny himself.   And in Romans it declares..........

Romans 3:3 For what if some did not believe? Shall their unbelief make the faith of God without effect?

All of the creation is sustained, maintained, and consists upon the reality of God having faith in **Himself**. We were created and made to walk in that realm of faith by trusting and having confidence, total reliance, complete dependence upon nothing but God. The only way the enemy could defeat man was by getting him out of the arena of faith. He had to sow the seed of unbelief into the soil of man's heart. Adam and his wife took the bait, thereby stepping out of the realm of faith, into a nightmare of death, poverty, fear, hate, lust, disobedience, sickness, and disease.

A Pandora's Box had been opened.

Christ Jesus came to shut that box, by bringing men back into a position of absolute total faith, confidence, trust, obedience and dependence upon God. Let's look at John 1:9 because within it is the evidence that at our conception God gave us faith.

John 1:9 That was the true Light, which lighteth <u>every man</u> that cometh into the world.

This light which lighteth up every man that comes into the world is the seed of faith, trust, and confidence in God. **Jesus** boldly declared that to enter into the kingdom of heaven, we must have the faith of a child! Everything that **Jesus** ever spoke was absolute truth. There was no exaggeration in anything he declared. Everything he spoke is the absolute, complete, and total truth. We can and must base our life totally upon what he declared!

Matthew 18:3 And said, Verily I say unto you, Except ye be converted, and become as little children, ye shall not enter into the kingdom of heaven.

Mark 10:15 Verily I say unto you, Whosoever shall not receive the kingdom of God as a little child, he shall not enter therein.

Luke 18:17 Verily I say unto you, Whosoever shall not receive the kingdom of God as a little child shall in no wise enter therein.

Jesus was declaring unless you once again have the faith of a little child (this is true conversion) you will never be able to enter in! We could look at all the attributes of a little child, which I believe is a natural manifestation of true faith in **Christ**! If you believe the Scripture I am about to share; It will clear up much confusion when it comes to those who have **not heard** the gospel. Please understand faith simply takes God at his word without any argument or doubting. *Romans 1:20-21 For the invisible things of him from the creation of the world are clearly seen, being understood by the things that are made, even his eternal power and Godhead; so that they are without excuse: [21] Because that, when they knew God, they glorified him not as God, neither were thankful; but became vain in their imaginations, and their foolish heart was darkened.*

Did you notice that it says that man is without excuse because at some time he understood? I know this sounds extremely strange, but it's true. Well, how would a child understand? Part of this mystery can be answered by Hebrews 11:3

Hebrews 11:3 Through faith we understand that the worlds were framed by the word of God so that things which are seen were not made of things which do appear.

When faith is alive and active, it understands, not with human reasoning, but from the inner depths of the heart. At the conception of every human being, there was this invisible substance called faith. Now the day came when a person knowingly, and willingly goes against the faith that is in his heart, thereby entering into a condition of what God calls death. Death is when you no longer have a pure, and holy faith in God out of the sincerity of your heart. It is when you willingly, and knowingly break the laws of God.

Remember when Mary told Elizabeth, her aunt that she was going to have a baby. That this baby was the son of God. What took place at that moment? It tells us that John within her womb, as an infant, leaped for joy. What caused this excitement in the heart of the unborn child John? He was **full of faith**. He understood in his mother's womb that **Jesus** was the son of God, the Lamb of God and that he had come to the Earth. This brought tremendous joy to his heart. This is another reason why he could be filled with the Spirit from his mother's womb because the Holy Ghost dwells in the atmosphere of faith.

Romans 7:9 For I was alive without the law once: but when the commandment came, sin revived, and I died.

Jesus Christ came to resurrect within the heart of every man **complete and absolute faith, trust, confidence, dependence, reliance, and obedience to God the Father**! Do not allow the enemy to tell you that you were born without faith. Faith is your natural habitat, dwelling place, just like the birds in the air, and the fish in the sea. Step back in to your rightful position.

It is important for us to understand that when we are born into this world that every part of our existence still needs to be developed. Whether it be our bones, muscles, organs, even our thinking and reasoning processes. **Even so, it is with Faith**. Our faith must be developed, grow, become strong. This particular book is dealing with the subject of healing, but I have written other books dealing with the subject of faith. One particular book that I have written is dealing with how your faith can grow, mature and be developed by 28 ways. **How Faith Comes!** I would strongly encourage you to purchase this book at Amazon. This book is available for free, or only $.99 as a Kindle book, or e-book. Here is a little explanation of what this book covers.

How Faith Comes! [28 WAYS THAT FAITH COMES!]

For over 40 years of Ministry, I probably have heard taught less than two biblical ways that faith comes. But in 2008 as I was in prayer early in the morning the Spirit of God opened up my understanding, instantly downloading into me 28 major ways of **HOW FAITH COMES** within three minutes. I sat down at the dinner table flabbergasted, taking a pen and paper, and writing down what the Lord showed me. It took me days to write what I had seen in about three minutes. This revelation continues to flow to this day giving me deeper understandings on the important subject of faith in **Christ**! The Lord showed me supernaturally and verified by Scriptures that there are approximately 28 ways that faith comes. This has been a progressive revelation. I am convinced that these are not the only ways that faith comes, but at this time it is the revelations that I have from God and his word.

How Faith Comes 28 Ways is not a new revelation, in the sense that it has always been there. Many of these 28 ways in which FAITH comes you will discover you have already been practicing, but now with a much clearer understanding, you will be able to exercise yourself in these ways in a more persistent way to develop your **FAITH in JESUS CHRIST**!

*18. The deliverance of Sarah of Tourette syndrome (1994)

Tourette syndrome (TS) is a neurological disorder characterized by repetitive, stereotyped, involuntary movements and vocalizations called tics. I am completely convinced that it is a demonic affliction. How many would make the mistake of thinking that someone with this syndrome is demon possessed, but they are oppressed! These demonic spirits, come and go, just like many people who have seizures. This is not a onetime pronouncement of deliverance. This is a true story of one young lady who was delivered by a progressive application of spiritual truths and authority.

Dr Michael H Yeager

Three months before school was out in 1994 I received a phone call from a husband and wife from Carlisle Pennsylvania. They called, asking if we could help them. They had been watching my TV program which was aired on their local TV station. They knew from my messages on TV that we had a Christian school. They had a daughter who was ten years old, who desperately needed help. Not only did she have tics syndrome, but she had major emotional problems.

The principle of the public school that she attended was demanding they place her in to a mental institution. She was completely uncontrollable. Whenever they would try to discipline her, she would run from them, many times ending up in the parking lot, crawling under the cars. One time when she was in the principal's office, Sarah got so angry, that she completely wiped out this office. They told me that she had gone completely berserk trashing everything in her sight. The principal of the school could not handle it anymore. The only other option this couple had was to see if somebody would take her into their school. Our school was over 30 miles away from where they lived, but they were willing to drive it every day. I told them that I would pray about it to see what the Lord spoke to me. I truly felt in my heart that we could help this young lady. A meeting was set up to meet the parents with their daughter Sarah.

I always like to pray before I make any commitments. I sought the Lord about this terrible situation with their daughter. As I spoke face-to-face with the parents, and with meeting Sarah for the first time, I perceived in my heart we could help her. First I told them that if we were going to help Sarah for the next three months, they would have to allow us to do what we felt needed to be done. The very first thing that they would need to do was to take Sarah off all mind altering drugs, which the public school had put her on. This is always one of our requirements for a child to come to our school. From 1985, up to this moment, in our school we never allowed any mind altering drugs. In every situation, we have seen God do marvelous things in a student's life.

The second thing I told the parents is that we would want them not to hang around at all at the school, once they drop their daughter off. I perceived by the spirit of God that a lot of Sarah's problem was that she was using her condition as a way to get attention from her mother and father. This proved to be correct, because every time her mother came to pick her up, the tics became much worse. When she first came to our school, her head would shake back and forth very violently all day long. It was extremely painful to watch.

I had a meeting with my teachers informing them that they were not to lift their voice, or yell at Sarah for any reason. We were not going to put her in a situation that would stir up the devils that were manifesting through her.

Many so-called Christians, especially the spirit filled ones, would have been trying to cast the devils out of her the minute they saw her because they would have thought she was demon possessed. Granted, there were devils at work, but she was not possessed. She was oppressed, depressed and at times obsessed. People who do not have a lot of wisdom immediately try to cast devils out without getting the mind of Christ.

The Spirit of God told me what we needed to do. Every morning when her mother dropped her off, I would take her with one of the female teachers of the school into an office. I would speak very softly to Sarah, telling her that we would like to pray with her before the beginning of the day. I would simply speak in a very soft voice over her that which was the will of God. This prayer would usually only be about five minutes long. Then I would tell her that she was going to have a wonderful day. Off to her class, she would go. We did not treat her any different than the other students. Through the day if they began to have problems with her, they would simply send someone to get me.

Once again we would take her into an office (with a lady teacher), and I would gently pray over her in the name of Jesus Christ. I also came against the demonic spirits that were causing the tics syndrome. I never got loud, authoritative, or weird. I would simply take authority over them, in a quiet, gentle voice.

Immediately there was a wonderful change in Sarah. Every day she was getting better. Not only did the tics syndrome cease eventually, but she became an A+ student. It was obvious to me at the beginning that Sarah was a brilliant girl, who was not being challenged at the school she attended.

By the end of the three months, Sarah was completely free. She was a happy, smiling, hard-working A+ student. We could not have asked for a better young girl. I am sorry to say that at the end of those three months we never saw Sarah or her parents again. I guess they had gotten what they needed, and off they went. This is very typical in my experience.

When the next school year rolled around, I received a very strange phone call one day from the Carlisle school district. The principal was on the phone wanting to talk to me. When I got on the phone with this principal, who was a lady, she asked me a question with a tone of absolute surprise and wonder. She said to me: what in the world did you do with Sarah? She is completely changed!

I said to this principal, who was over a large school district, "What we did with Sarah you're not going to be able to do!" I said to her: we began to pray over her very gently, every day, consistently in the name of Jesus Christ. You could hear a pin drop for the next couple moments. The next thing I heard was, OH, okay, goodbye! The principal hung up the phone!

*19. A Sad but True Story! (1999)

I had a former pastor one time that leads a rebellion against me in our Christian school and our church. This gentleman had been one of the teachers in our school for some years (he had also been a pastor of a local church) and because of a decision I had made he had become extremely angry and upset at me. He was so upset at me that he spoke to all of our school teachers, and our personnel against me.

This bitterness in his heart spread like a house on fire throughout the whole ministry. Strife, gossip, and rumors about me began to spread like an incurable disease. It became so bad that after the school year, I simply had to shut the school down. I mean it was so vicious that it was impossible to keep going with our school.

James 3:16 For where envying and strife are, there are confusion and every evil work.

During this whole conflict, not one time did I ever get angry, bitter or upset with him knowing that I could not afford to be bitter. The next thing that I heard was that this dear brother had been hit with a deadly and incurable disease. I began earnestly praying for him, he had been a good pastor and teacher at one time but had allowed the seed of bitterness to spring up in him, contaminating many others with him. One day out of the blue I received a phone call from this man's wife.

She said her husband would like to speak to me. I had to press the phone tightly against my ear because he was speaking to me with barely a whisper. He asked me to please forgive him for what he had done. He said he knew he was wrong for causing all of the strife which he had caused. With tears rolling down my face I told him that he was forgiven. We had spoken for a little bit longer before we both hung up. Late that same evening he passed on to be with the Lord. Praise God for his mercy and his goodness that even when we disobey him, there is still **mercy** and forgiveness available.

Hebrews 12:15 Looking diligently lest any man fails of the grace of God; lest any root of bitterness springing up trouble you, and thereby many be defiled;

We have to be careful that a root of bitterness is not allowed in any of us. It is a demonic seed of unbelief which rises up against the mercy of God that we must operate in for other people, whether they are right or wrong.

CHAPTER EIGHT

#3 Eat & Drink the Word

The Bible says in the last days that there is going to be a famine in the land. In my opinion, this famine has already been manifested, and it is a famine of God's word hidden in the heart of believers. Many believers do not understand God. They do not know how to trust God, or to look to God because there has been a lack of those in leadership who move in the realm of faith and the word. Much of the modern church leaders are successful not because of faith in **Christ, and God's word**, but simply because they are worldly wise. Using natural, practical worldly wisdom to grow their local churches, and yet the Scripture declares that ***man shall not live by bread alone, but by every word that proceeds out of the mouth of God.***

MOST OF THOSE WE HAVE CALLED SUCCESSFUL PASTORS ARE SIMPLY WORLDLY WISE MAN. TRUE SUCCESS IS WHEN WE SEE THE IMAGE & CHARACTER OF CHRIST BEING FORMED IN PEOPLE!

Proverbs 3:5-6 Trust in the Lord with all thine heart; and lean not unto thine own understanding. In all thy ways acknowledge him, and he shall direct thy paths.

If you read Hebrews 11, there is 50 events in this particular chapter. We call this chapter the Faith Hall of Fame. We need to take really a good look at these men and women, and the conditions that they were experiencing. How they responded to all of these trials, tribulations, and test. They overcame **by faith based upon the word that God** had given to them. It is a faith that works by love, and when you are walking in this realm of faith you will not worry, you will not be fearful, you will not be angry, you will not be frustrated, you will not be upset, you will not be self-centered, you will not be self-serving and self-seeking, you will not be self-pleasing! True biblical faith takes a hold of God's word, and the divine nature of **Christ,** and will not let go. When **Jesus** said that faith had made a person whole, what he was saying is your confidence in me, in my word, and your confidence in **My Father** has made you whole. So it's your faith in **these three areas** that makes all things possible. The **third step, realm, reality that must be in our life to bring deliverance** is that we must eat and drink the **Word of God.** We must eat and drink the words of Christ, even as the descendants of Abraham partook of the Passover Lamb.

John 6:1 After these things Jesus went over the sea of Galilee, which is the sea of Tiberias.² And a great multitude followed him because they saw his miracles which he did on them that were diseased.³ And Jesus went up into a mountain, and there he sat with his disciples.⁴ And the passover, a feast of the Jews, was nigh.'

The **Passover** is indeed the most important festival, feast day, tradition and ceremony of the Jewish people. To better comprehend exactly what the **Passover** is, we would have to step back into history and take a look in the book of Exodus when God had sent Moses to deliver the Israelites from the hands of Pharaoh.

God sent Moses to the Israelites to bring deliverance and freedom because they have been in captivity for 400 years. Of course, Moses is a typology of **Jesus Christ** who came to set us free from the slavery of sin by or through the means of us having faith in **Christ, and his word.** God told Pharaoh through Moses to let his people go. We all know the story how Pharaoh refused to obey God. The Lord had Moses to bring plague after plague to free the people from the hands of Pharaoh. None of these plagues convinced Pharaoh to lose God's people. There was to be one last judgment, and It was the **Passover lamb.** This would be the final blow to Egypt which would release the children of God, by and through the **Passover** God would change the world. From that moment forward nothing would ever be the same. As you and I receive revelation on the **Passover**, and what it means to us, our lives will never be the same. The **Passover** in the Bible is talked about specifically **73 times**. It talks about the **lamb** or the **Passover lamb one hundred times.** As a result of the Passover, the children of Israel from that day forward (if they would believe the words of Moses) could walk in health, and receive divine healing.

Psalm 105:37 He brought them forth also with silver and gold: and there was not one feeble person among their tribes.

Exodus 15:26 And said, If thou wilt diligently hearken to the voice of the Lord thy God, and wilt do that which is right in his sight, and wilt gives ear to his commandments, and keep all his statutes, I will put none of these diseases upon thee, which I have brought upon the Egyptians: for I am the Lord that healeth thee.

Did you notice that God told Moses that everyone should go and get themselves a lamb without spot or blemish? The Lord told Moses that if you obey me in the keeping of this celebration, it will finally set you **free from the control of the enemy**! If we as believers would do likewise, with the revelation of **Christ** our **Passover lamb**, we would truly be set free and set people free. What is the **3rd Step** in our preparation in setting people free?

#3 By Eating & Drinking Jesus Christ and the word of God!

Hebrews 11:28 Through faith he kept the passover, and the sprinkling of blood, lest he that destroyed the firstborn should touch them.

Deliverance comes when you eat of the **Passover** using God's **WORD**, with a sincere heart of love and devotion. Of course, the **Passover lamb** is **Jesus Christ**, the only begotten Son of God. John the Baptist had a revelation of **Jesus Christ**. When he was baptizing at the river Jordan, and John saw **Jesus** walking towards him, he said: **Behold the Lamb of God Which Takes Away the Sins of the World!**

Now there were conditions that had to be met for the people to have a right to partake of the **Passover lamb**, and to protect them from the Death Angel which was going to pass through the land. Everyone must be dressed ready to leave; the **blood** had to be applied to the door post and the lintel which is symbolic of our thought life and the works of the flesh. All of the men had to be physical circumcised.

To do the **Passover** justice, we would have to look at every spiritual truth, lesson that is wrapped up in the **Passover,** which in itself would easily become a book. Suffice it to say that as we partake of the bread, the grape juice as **Jesus** commanded us, recognizing by faith that it is his body, his blood which he gave for our salvation; faith will begin to rise in our hearts for our deliverance, and the deliverance of others. In the Garden of Gethsemane **Jesus** said to the Father: if at all possible let this cup pass from me, but not my will be done, let your will be done. The cup he was speaking about was the cup of cursing. In the old covenant, it talks about the curse placed upon sinful flesh. **Jesus Christ** became a curse for us that we might be made free from the curse of the law.[47] **All the congregation of Israel shall keep it.** Everyone that names the name of **Christ** is required to keep the **Passover**. I am not referring to the one that was observed in Exodus, but the one that **Christ** declares today.

John 6:.48 I am that bread of life.49 Your fathers did eat manna in the wilderness and are dead.50 This is the bread which cometh down from heaven, that a man may eat thereof, and not die.51 I am the living bread which came down from heaven: if any man eats of this bread, he shall live for ever: and the bread that I will give is my flesh, which I will give for the life of the world....[55] For my flesh is meat indeed, and my blood is drink indeed.[56] He that eateth my flesh and drinketh my blood, dwelleth in me, and I in him.[57] As the living Father hath sent me,

and I live by the Father: so he that eateth me, even he shall live by me.

As we have intimacy with **Christ,** we will come into oneness with **Jesus Christ and his word.** Now we can never over emphasize the need to apprehend and the development of our faith in **Christ.** The growing, developing and increasing of our faith is extremely important to our success in bringing the **FREEDOM** to all that we minister to. Everything that we have, everything that we partake of in **Christ** has to be done by faith. All things were created by God, by faith. God created all things by having faith in himself! Believers are those who do not trust in themselves, but we trust and faith in God.

Psalm 37:5 Commit thy way unto the Lord; trust also in him; and he shall bring it to pass.

Jesus said that at the very end of the ages, right before he came back, would be there any faith left on the earth? The faith that we are talking about is a faith that apprehends the character, nature, the mind, the heart, and the will of God. A faith that takes a hold of **Jesus Christ,** and brings the believer into a place of victory over sin, the world, the flesh, sickness, disease, infirmities, and the devil. Faith is just like the physical muscles in your body. A lot of people are out of shape physically in America. It is not because we they have any fewer muscles then other previous generations. We have the same muscles that our parents, grandparents, or are great-great-grandparents had. Most people are simply out of shape because they are not exercising their natural muscles. They are not eating the proper type of foods. The natural world is symbolic of what's going on in the spiritual world. People spiritually are not exercising their faith, and they are not eating the proper spiritual foods.

1 Timothy 4:8 For bodily exercise profiteth little: but godliness is profitable unto all things, having the promise of the life that now is, and of that which is to come.

#4. Be Extremely Serious!

The fourth step in bringing is that you must become very serious about helping people. You must even go beyond the word serious to the place of truly meaning business, or you could say: **get to the point of being desperate.** Yes, you must become desperate to set others free, desperate to bring deliverance, desperate to see people made whole.

The Bible says the kingdom of heaven suffers violence, and the violent take it by force.

I want you to know that you **MUST** be serious, you have got to mean business. The major problem is that many Christians take the pathway of least resistance. It is so easy just to run off to the world and to get their help, and it is very easy just to run off to the doctors. It's easy to trust in the arm of the flesh. Please do not misunderstand me with the statements I am making. Truly I am not attacking people who use the world, but I'm simply stating the fact that in the midst of running to the world, instead of looking to God, we are tying the hands of God, and cutting our selves off from a Miracle. There are many scriptures that deal with not trusting God, and trusting man instead.

Jeremiah 17:5 Thus saith the Lord; Cursed be the man that trusteth in man, and maketh flesh his arm, and whose heart departeth from the Lord.

Psalm 118:8 It is better to trust in the Lord than to put confidence in man. 9 It is better to trust in the Lord than to put confidence in princes.

Isaiah 2:22 Cease ye from man, whose breath is in his nostrils: for wherein is he to be accounted of

Psalm 146:3 Put not your trust in princes, nor in the son of man, in whom there is no help. 4 His breath goeth forth, he returneth to his earth; in that very day, his thoughts perish.

2 Chronicles 32:8 With him is an arm of flesh, but with us is the Lord our God to help us, and to fight our battles. And the people rested themselves upon the words of Hezekiah king of Judah.

Isaiah 31:1 Woe to them that go down to Egypt for help; and stay on horses, and trust in chariots, because they are many; and in horsemen, because they are very strong, but they look not unto the Holy One of Israel, neither seek the Lord!

God wants us to trust Him, God wants us to come to Him, God wants to help us, God wants us to believe him, but He is not going to make you. The **fourth step** you must take is you have to become serious, very serious; you could even say desperate when it comes to being used of God. **Pacifism** will open the door for the devil to possibly killing you when it comes to casting out devils. There is no room for pacifism in this fight of faith because we are not dealing with flesh and blood, but **principalities, and powers, rulers of darkness, and spiritual wickedness in high places**. The thief, the devil has come to steal, kill, and to destroy you.

Acts 10:38 How God anointed Jesus of Nazareth with the Holy Ghost and with power: who went about doing good, and healing all that were oppressed of the devil; for God was with him.

We see many illustrations throughout the Scriptures of people getting serious about being free, deliverance, or healing, and not one of them did God disappoint! In the book of Revelation when Christ was speaking to the church, he said he was not happy with them because they were lukewarm. They were lackadaisical, lay back, take it, easy pacifist. He said because they were neither cold, nor hot, but because they were lukewarm, he would vomit them out of his mouth. As long as you are lukewarm in your attitude towards your healing, it will be very difficult for you to receive your miracle. I would strongly encourage you to read these three events that occurred in the Gospels.

The first event was a woman with an issue of blood, who pressed her way through the masses to get healed. The second event is about blind Bartimaeus. Even with the disciples of Jesus telling him to be quiet, he would not shut up until he had received from Christ that which he believed for. The third event is about a **Phoenician woman whose daughter needed to be delivered from demons**. In this particular situation, it would even appear that Jesus spoke words that were very offensive. The woman did not allow this to discourage her, but pressed in until Jesus answer her prayers, and **her daughter was delivered**. This is so vitally important when it comes to us receiving our healing, which Christ has already purchased for us.

Matthew 9:20 And, behold, a woman, which was diseased with an issue of blood twelve years, came behind him and touched the hem of his garment:21 For she said within herself, If I may but touch his garment, I shall be whole.22 But Jesus turned him about, and when he saw her, he said, Daughter, be of good comfort; thy faith hath made thee whole. And the woman was made whole from that hour.

Mark 10:46 And they came to Jericho: and as he went out of Jericho with his disciples and a great number of people, blind Bartimaeus, the son of Timaeus, sat by the highway side begging.47 And when he heard that it was Jesus of Nazareth, he began to cry out, and say, Jesus, thou son of David, have mercy on me. 48 And many charged him that he should hold his peace: but he cried the more a great deal, Thou son of David, have mercy on me. 49 And Jesus stood still and commanded him to be called. And they call the blind man, saying unto him, Be of good comfort, rise; he calleth thee. 50 And he, casting away his garment, rose, and came to Jesus. 51 And Jesus answered and said unto him, What wilt thou that I should do unto thee? The blind man said unto him, Lord, that I might receive my sight. 52 And Jesus said unto him, Go thy way; thy faith hath made thee whole. And immediately he received his sight and followed Jesus in the way.

Matthew 15:21 Then Jesus went thence, and departed into the coasts of Tyre and Sidon.22 And, behold, a woman of Canaan came out of the same coasts, and cried unto him, saying, Have mercy on me, O Lord, thou son of David; my daughter is grievously vexed with a devil.23 But he answered her not a word. And his disciples came and besought him, saying, Send her away; for she crieth after us.24 But he answered and said, I am not sent but unto the lost sheep of the house of Israel.25 Then came she and worshipped him, saying, Lord, help me.26 But he answered and said, It is not meet to take the children's bread, and to cast it to dogs.27 And she said, Truth, Lord: yet the dogs eat of the crumbs which fall from their masters' table.28 Then Jesus answered and said unto her, O woman, great is thy faith: be it unto thee even as thou wilt. And her daughter was made whole from that very hour.

This is a mystery of active and living faith in Christ being manifested in a person's life. If you are really serious and desperate, you will be a be a doer of taking a hold of God and not letting go. Even in the world success is only achieved by those who are truly and extremely serious about what they are involved in. It is God's will to bring deliverance to you, and healing to you, but it will take a **violent faith**. I have run into many believers who have a twisted, perverted view when it comes to casting out devils. They get caught up in weird, mystical methods! I hope you realize that the salvation and freedom which Christ has purchased for us was not easily accomplished, or cheaply bought. When Jesus said:

John 14:12 Verily, verily, I say unto you, He that believeth on me, the works that I do shall he do also; and greater works than these shall he do; because I go unto my Father.

The works he was referring to was the aggressive, violent, and desperate acts of faith that he accomplished, with him even going all the way to the whipping post, the cross, and the grave. He had determined in his heart that he would obey the Father in that which he was asked to do until its ultimate conclusion.

Isaiah 50:7 For the Lord God will help me; therefore shall I not be confounded: therefore have I set my face like a flint, and I know that I shall not be ashamed.

I have seen many people set free in the last 40 years by aggressively taking a hold of God, and not letting go. You have to take the bull by the horns, put the ax to the grinding wheel, make the dust fly if you're going to set people free. I am amazed at what people allow the medical world to do to them so that they might be made whole. If we would only turn all of this desperation, this overwhelming seriousness towards the Lord, I believe we would see many more miracles, deliverances, healing in our lives. God had given the children of Israel the land that flowed with milk and honey, but did you notice that they had to fight for it. Paul, the apostle, said he had fought a good fight, and that he had finished his course. There must be a faith in your heart that rises and takes a hold of God's promises when it comes to divine healing.

For over 40 years I have aggressively, violently, and persistently taken a hold of Gods will. I refuse to let the devil rob me of what Jesus so painfully purchased. It is mine, and the devil cannot have it. The thought has never even entered my mind to see a doctor when physical sickness attacked my body. You see I already have a doctor; his name is Jesus Christ of Nazareth. He is the great physician, and he has already healed me with his stripes. Yes, there has been times when the manifestation of my healing seemed like it would never come, but I knew, that I knew, that I knew by his stripes I was healed. Strong faith never considers the circumstances.

#5 Never Exalt The Devil!

The fifth step in God using you to bring deliverance or to be delivered is that you **must never, never, ever** exalt the devil, evil manifestations, the negative circumstances, the symptoms in the victim. **What do I mean by this statement?** I hear many Christians exalting the devil or their problems, and yet I have personally known believers that had major problems, but never talked about them, never made a big deal out of them, never even told people what they were going through.

We need to see people begin to rise up in faith, and go after the will of God. When faith is in operation, it will cause you to pray, gathered together with the Saints, meditate upon Gods word, deny your flesh, shares your faith with others, and take care of the needy. We have lost our faith in **Christ** in America, and yet there is still great hope because our faith can be restored in **Christ**. God desires us to have great faith to bring deliverance, and he has provided for us many different ways to acquire it. All of these blessings, provisions and protections will be activated in our life as we are **dwelling** and **abiding** in **Jesus**.

2 Timothy 1:7 For God hath not given us the spirit of fear, but of power, and of love, and of a sound mind.

There is no fear of what men will do to you, or of sickness, or disease, or poverty, or financial lack, or plagues, or afflictions, or demonic spirits. There is no fear; there is no worry, and there is no torment when we are walking in the realm of faith, based upon the will, and the word of God. You will have peace that passes all understanding, joy unspeakable, and full of glory. When somebody is sick in the natural, we can put our hands on their fore head to see if they are running a fever. The doctor can have you open your mouth, and he will look at your tonsils or your tongue.

Symptoms in your physical body will reveal sickness by certain manifestations. This is also true when it comes to divine faith. If you are truly operating in faith, the divine attributes of **Christ** will be manifested. The nine fruits of the spirit should be evident. You will be living a holy separated, consecrated life for God. If you are not, then it is evidence that you need to step back into that realm of faith by eating and drinking Jesus Christ, and meditating upon God's word.

One time when Smith Wigglesworth (who was an amazing man of Faith) had a real serious financial situation, he went to pray for a wealthy man. When he prayed for this wealthy man, the man was gloriously healed, and delivered right then and there! The wealthy man told Smith Wigglesworth that he wanted to bless him, asking if there was anything he could do to help him? He told the wealthy man: No brother, but thanked him any ways for the offer. Smith was looking to God to take care of a desperate financial need. By the way, God did do an amazing miracle to meet this financial need.

On another occasion, Smith Wigglesworth ended up with a terrible affliction of gallstones. When he was informed by a specialist that the only way of deliverance from these gallstones was by an operation, Smith Wigglesworth responded with:

"God Shall Operate"

His son-in-law, James Salter, said that during the whole three years of this trial, Smith never stopped preaching, never complained, or told anyone. Even though Smith Wigglesworth was in great pain, and bled a great deal, he continued to minister to the sick, even with blood running down his legs, filling his socks and shoes, as he laid hands on the sick. He did end up spend many days in bed in great pain, but would get up to make it to the meetings where he was to minister. This test supposedly went on the day, after day, after another day, and night, after night.

It is reported that the meetings he conducted during this time were powerful, with many attesting to the wonderful miracles of God's healing power. When deliverance finally manifested in Smith Wigglesworth body, which was almost instantaneous, with all of the gallstones, 20 or more coming out. Smith Wigglesworth was made completely and perfectly whole. Smith put those stones in a small tin can and on occasions he would show the stones to different people as he told them of Gods faithfulness. Some of these stones were quite large: others were jagged and needle shaped. All of the stones not only caused tremendous pain but penetrated his innards in such a way that it caused constant hemorrhaging. Smith was a man who understood what it meant to have faith that worked by patients. He had an unshakable faith that caused him to agree with God, and to disagree with the circumstances no matter the pain, or problem.

Whenever we exalt the devil, sickness, the afflictions or the problems of our lives, we are operating in a spirit of unbelief. I am not saying that we cannot share privately with people of faith what we are going through so that they can agree and believe with us. In over 40 years of walking with Christ, personally, I have shared very little with people what I was being confronted with. I knew that most people were not truly going to be believing with me, but would simply tell others what I was going through. I would like to share with you one examples of this in the four Gospels, in the ministry of Jesus. The first one we need to look at is the father who had a demon possessed son.

Mark 9:17 And one of the multitude answered and said, Master, I have brought unto thee my son, which hath a dumb spirit; 18 And wheresoever he taketh him, he teareth him: and he foameth, and gnasheth with his teeth, and pineth away: and I spake to thy disciples that they should cast him out; and they could not.

19 He answereth him, and saith, O faithless generation, how long shall I be with you? How long shall I suffer you? bring him unto me. 20 And they brought him unto him: and when he saw him, straightway the spirit tare him; and he fell on the ground, and wallowed foaming. 21 And he asked his father, How long is it ago since this came unto him? And he said, Of a child. 22 And oft times it hath cast him into the fire, and into the waters, to destroy him: but if thou canst do anything, have compassion on us, and help us. 23 Jesus said unto him, If thou canst believe, all things are possible to him that believeth. 24 And straightway the father of the child cried out, and said with tears, Lord, I believe; help thou mine unbelief. 25 When Jesus saw that the people came running together, he rebuked the foul spirit, saying unto him, Thou dumb and deaf spirit, I charge thee, come out of him, and enter no more into him. 26 And the spirit cried, and rent him sore, and came out of him: and he was as one dead; insomuch that many said, He is dead. 27 But Jesus took him by the hand, and lifted him up; and he arose.

In this particular incident, I want you to notice how the father was more than **willing to brag about the demonic afflictions** that were upon his son. Jesus **never asked people what was wrong with them**, but would ask them what it was that they wanted. In most of these situations, it was obvious what the people needed, but he would ask them what it was they wanted. In **Mark 11: 24** Jesus said: **Whatsoever things you desire, when you pray, believe that you receive, and you shall have.** Jesus was always directing the needy to ask for what they needed, and **not to meditate upon the problem.**

On many occasions when Jesus was surrounded by people who were boasting on the devil, he would direct the needy away from them. We had the one illustration of this when the couple's daughter died! Let's take a moment to look at this particular Scripture.

Matthew 9:18 While he spake these things unto them, behold, there came a certain ruler, and worshipped him, saying, My daughter is even now dead: but come and lay thy hand upon her, and she shall live.19 And Jesus arose, and followed him, and so did his disciples....... 23 And when Jesus came into the ruler's house and saw the minstrels and the people making a noise,24 He said unto them, Give place: for the maid is not dead, but

*sleepeth. And they laughed him to scorn.25 **But when the
people were put forth,** he went in, and took her by the hand,
and the maid arose.*

Understand that none of us have arrived, and none of us are
walking in 100% faith all the time. Sometimes I get out of the will
of God, I panic, I look at the circumstances, I look at the problem.
As I share these truths with you, I am not claiming that I have
arrived. I am simply coming from the place in which I have had
many experiences, many wonderful results by simply following the
principles (not a formula) of the word of God. **We must never
boast, never brag, never exalt the devil, and never exalt the
circumstance that is contrary to the word of God.** I can give
you a lot of examples found in the Bible when men and women
contradicted Gods word and exalted the problem, and it never
ended well for them.

In Numbers 13 we discover a powerful illustration of this
when the spies went into the land of promise that God had
proclaimed flowed with milk and honey. When the 12 spies
returned, they acknowledged that what God said was true.

*Numbers 13:27 And they told him, and said, We came unto the
land whither thou sentest us, and surely it floweth with milk and
honey, and this is the fruit of it.*

Now, it is wonderful that they acknowledged that what God
said is true, yet in their next words they demean the promise, and
called God a liar, and that his promise of protecting and providing
for them false. They exalted their enemies above God.

*Numbers 13:28 Nevertheless the people be strong that dwell in
the land and the cities are walled, and very great: and moreover
we saw the children of Anak there.29 The Amalekites dwell in
the land of the south: and the Hittites, and the Jebusites, and the
Amorites, dwell in the mountains: and the Canaanites dwell by
the sea, and by the coast of Jordan.*

This information that they began to spew forth was nothing new. God had already informed them about the enemy, with all of their tribal names, and at the same time, he told them that their enemies would be bread for them to eat. Joshua and Caleb spoke up in the mist of their declaration, and declared that God was more than able if they would simply look to him, they would be able to overcome. If you read the context of this whole story, you will sadly discover that they rose up against these two men of faith, against God, against Moses, and in a violent manner. They said that they would rather have stayed in Egypt, or died in the wilderness then go back into Canaan to overcome the enemy. God granted their wish by allowing the first generation out of Egypt to die in the desert.

I run into believers all the time, Christians, not sinners that have made devils, demons, the problems they are dealing with, sicknesses and diseases in their bodies, in their minds bigger than God.

Now how can it be that the God who upholds all things with the power of his word is not able to overcome the problems of our life? From Genesis, all the way to the end of the book of Revelation God reveals himself as more than enough in every situation. Every trial, every affliction, every test simply reveals how big you have made God in your life.

The question we all need to ask ourselves is: **How Big Is Our God?** It reminds me of the biblical story of David and Goliath. The Israel Army was confronted by the Philistines, who had a champion by the name of Goliath. Goliath had for 40 days challenged anybody to face him, but there were none in Israel's army that had enough faith in God to face him.

1 Samuel 17:4 And there went out a champion out of the camp of the Philistines, named Goliath, of Gath, whose height was six cubits and a span......10 And the Philistine said, I defy the armies of Israel this day; give me a man, that we may fight together.11 When Saul and all Israel heard those words of the Philistine, they were dismayed, and greatly afraid........16 And the Philistine drew near morning and evening, and presented himself forty days........

Here comes along a Shepherd boy by the name of David that says: who is this uncircumcised Philistine that should defy the armies of the living God? Now you have a whole army of men exalting their enemy, Goliath by name, and you have one young shepherd boy by the name of David saying: this man is nothing compared to my God. It might have sounded like David was just full of pride, but in reality, it was faith speaking, because not only did he declare that Goliath was nobody, and nothing, but that he would be willing to face this man. I have met many believers who talk a big talk but have little corresponding action.

Faith, when it is in operation, will never exalt, brag, or magnify that which is against the will of God. I hear believers all the time exalting their problems, their sicknesses, their afflictions, and their symptoms. When you are truly operating in faith, you will only, and always exalt God, and his word. This is a tremendous way that I have discovered to find out **if I'm truly operating in faith.** My mouth gives me a way all the time, it reveals to myself where I am at. There is a tremendous Scripture given to us in the book of James about this reality.

James 1:22 But be ye doers of the word, and not hearers only, deceiving your own selves.23 For if any be a hearer of the word, and not a doer, he is like unto a man beholding his natural face in a glass:24 For he beholdeth himself, and goeth his way, and straightway forgetteth what manner of man he was.25 But whoso looketh into the perfect law of liberty, and continueth therein, he being not a forgetful hearer, but a doer of the work, this man shall be blessed in his deed.

The enemy loves to turn a molehill into a mountain, which we ignorantly and innocently begin to confess over our lives. Now even if it is truly a mountain God tells us that we can speak to the mountain and cast it into the sea. Never allow the devil to get you to exalt the demonic manifestations, sickness, disease, or afflictions in your body or others.

Shut Up and Come Out

When I deal with demonic powers, I tell them **to shut up and come out** of the victim. I do not put up with evil spirits doing strange manifestations. Many people who are involved in the so-called deliverance ministry want to see manifestations of the devil. They do not know what spirit that they are of. Personally, I'm not messing around with the enemy, and I do not need to be entertained by their contortions horrendous evil and hideous phenomenon. Yes, in 40 years I have seen some strange things, but I do not put up with it! It is a part of the fallen nature in people that loves to see evil and all of its twisted shenanigans. The enemies of our soul, *which are the enemies of God*, love to be exalted and magnified. It is the same when it comes to healing. People will experience a symptom in their body (given to them by the devil), and they will begin to give their time, attention, energy, money, mind and emotions to those symptoms. The enemy rejoices in this and then will manifest himself even more through this symptom. All of a sudden more symptoms will come because we've given place to the devil. I simply tell the symptoms to **shut up, the spirit of infirmity come out, and be gone.** Then I go on about my business. For over 40 years this is my routine in how I treat the devil and his lies.

I have purposely strived never to exalt the problem I'm experiencing, even if I'm not operating in faith. There is a Scripture in Ephesians that encourages us never to speak that which is contrary to God's word.

Ephesians 4:29 Let no corrupt communication proceed out of your mouth, but that which is good to the use of edifying, that it may minister grace unto the hearers.

There is another set of scriptures discovered in Philippians 4 that also encourages us along the same line.

Philippians 4:8 Finally, brethren, whatsoever things are true, whatsoever things are honest, whatsoever things are just, whatsoever things are pure, whatsoever things are lovely, whatsoever things are of good report; if there be any virtue, and if there be any praise, think on these things.

We are living in a time when many believer's faith is so weak that they spend all of their time exalting their problems, exalting afflictions, exalting the infirmities in their body, exalting evil. The purpose of writing this book is not to demean people, but to help them come to the place of strong faith in Christ Jesus, to where they can be used of God in ~~sending~~ setting people free. We need to realize that the devil loves it when we are speaking death over ourselves and others. Negative words will draw demonic powers right to us.

I remember as a young boy sitting around a campfire late at night, and somebody would be sharing a terrible, dreadful, frightening story. In every one of these situations my heart began to be filled with great fear and dread, because unknown to us that as we were **exalting demonic activities, it brought us demonic powers**. The opposite is also true when we begin to exalt Christ, God, and his word. As we begin to exalt the truth, the truth will draw God's divine presence to us, his power, his angelic beings, because Angels hearken to the voice of God's word!

Psalm 103:20 Bless the Lord, ye his angels, that excel in strength, that do his commandments, hearkening unto the voice of his word.

Psalm 81:13 Oh that my people had hearkened unto me, and Israel had walked in my ways! 14 I should soon have subdued their enemies, and turned my hand against their adversaries.

James 4:8 Draw nigh to God, and he will draw nigh to you.
Cleanse your hands, ye sinners; and purify your hearts, ye
double minded.

Now please take heed to this spiritual truth, and whether
you accept it, or not, this is absolute truth. In this world, flowers
will draw to themselves honeybees, even as manure always draws
flies. The word of God spoken out of your mouth, from your heart
will always bring God's angels, God's presence, and God's power!
Jesus said to the devil: **"It Is Written"** three times, in which
immediately angelic beings appeared to minister to him.

Matthew 4:11 Then the devil leaveth him, and, behold, angels
came and ministered unto him.

Angel appeared and strengthened him when he was in a
garden of Gethsemane praying that the heavenly Father's will
would be accomplished in his life, instead of his own.

Luke 22:43 And there appeared an angel unto him from heaven,
strengthening him.

Even as angelic beings hearken to the voice of God as you
speak the word, so do demons respond when you exalt the devil,
when you exalt demonic activities, sickness, or when you exalt
diseases. People hear the word **cancer**, and it fills their heart with
absolute fear. The Scriptures boldly declare that fear has torment
and that it is not of God. *God has not given us a spirit of fear, but*
of power, love, and a sound mind. On three different occasions, I
had the symptoms of cancer in my body. There were times when I
had extremely painful tumors. On another occasion, I had what
appeared to be prostate cancer. One of my longest battles was
when all indications declared that I had colon cancer. But by faith
in Christ, I'm still alive, vibrant and well.

1 John 5:4 For whatsoever is born of God overcometh the
world: and this is the victory that overcometh the world, even
our faith.

CHAPTER NINE

#6 Examine Your Heart

The **sixth step, reality, truth** that you need to embrace to be used of God and bring in deliverance to others is to examine your own heart. We need to make sure that we are not involved in **known sin, rebellion, disobedience to God**. We also need to make sure that there is not any **bitterness, resentment, on ᴇ̶ʀ̶ un forgiveness, or hatred in our hearts**. I am not speaking about being sinless, or even confessing that your sinless. The only sinless man that has ever walked this earth was Jesus Christ. In first John it says:

1 John 1:7 But if we walk in the light, as he is in the light, we have fellowship one with another, and the blood of Jesus Christ his Son cleanseth us from all sin. 8 If we say that we have no sin, we deceive ourselves, and the truth is not in us. 9 If we confess our sins, he is faithful and just to forgive us our sins, and to cleanse us from all unrighteousness.

I am speaking about **open rebellion to God**. I'm saying if you're going to have full confidence in your prayers being answered, in casting out Devils, you must make sure that your heart is right with God. If you discover that there are things in your life that are contrary to God's will when it comes to your own personal decisions, then you simply need to repent, confess your sins to Christ, and turn away from your wicked deeds. God will be faithful, and just to forgive you of all of your unrighteousness.

Once you confess and repent of your sins, do not think for a moment that automatically the enemy will leave you alone. The demonic world is similar to that of nasty little gnats swarming around your head constantly aggravating, and attacking you. It is like when you or I am walking through woods a forest in the summertime. Before you know what is happening these pesky, nasty little gnats, horse flies begin to show up buzzing around your head. These nasty little insects just will not leave you alone, especially when you're sweating, or you're out there splitting wood. You cannot go by how you feel when you are standing on God's word for your Forgiveness, and your Healing.

The enemy will tell you that God has not forgiven you even though you have repented, confessed, and turned away from the sins in the sincerity of your heart. I tell people it is like a skunk that has been killed. The skunk is dead, but the stink will still hang around for a while. After you have examined your heart and confessed your sins, then you can come **boldly** before the throne of grace in your time of need to obtain mercy, and find grace to help in overcoming these sins.

Hebrews 4:15 For we have not a high priest which cannot be touched with the feeling of our infirmities; but was in all points tempted like as we are, yet without sin.16 Let us, therefore, come boldly unto the throne of grace, that we may obtain mercy, and find grace to help in time of need.

One of the greatest attributes of God is that he is merciful, and his mercy is new every morning. The **sixth step, reality, the truth** is that you must examine your heart making sure there is no sin in your heart, no bitterness, no resentment, no hate towards anyone that might have hurt you in any way, or your loved ones. This is a very serious area that must be dealt with in our lives. You see God boldly declares that if you do not forgive others, then God will not forgive you.

Matthew 6:15 But if ye forgive not men their trespasses, neither will your Father forgive your trespasses.

The Scriptures dealing with the subject of forgiveness, and forgiving others must be taken very seriously.

God means what he says, and says what he means!

Never think for a moment that because God is love, and is full of compassion, and mercy that it overrides what he has proclaimed, declared as truth. Based upon the reality of the Scriptures we can see immediately that the doctrine of Calvinism, OSAS, (Once Saved Always Saved) Is a deception propagated by the devil. Un-forgiveness in our hearts is a decision that we make. We knowingly, and purposely choose not to forgive someone who has done us wrong, or we believe they have committed a wrong. God boldly declares that he is the only one that has the right not to forgive.

Luke 6:37 Judge not, and ye shall not be judged: condemn not, and ye shall not be condemned: forgive, and ye shall be forgiven:

You might say that un-forgiveness is the unpardonable sin, that is until you forgive from the heart. Now, this is very serious because God says **if you do not forgive** from your heart, then all of **your sins are placed back onto you**. Basically, if you do not forgive from your heart *THEN* ~~than~~ what Christ did on the cross for you, absolutely will not help you in any regards. This truth will set you free from the deception of Calvinism, and Antinomianism. A person who sins are not forgiven cannot, and will not go to heaven!

Matthew 18:34 And his lord was wroth, and delivered him to the tormentors, till he should pay all that was due unto him.35 So likewise shall my heavenly Father also do unto you, if ye from your hearts forgive not everyone his brother their trespasses.

SMITHS WIGGLESWORTH RESPONSE TO CALVINISM

God says to us, "In patience possess thy soul." How beautiful! There have been in England great churches which believed once saved always saved. I thank God that they are all disappearing. You will find if you go to England those hardheaded people that used to hold on to these things are almost gone. Why? Because they went on to say whatever you did, if you were elect, you were right. That is so wrong. **The elect of God is those that keep pressing forward**. The elect of God cannot hold still. They are always on the move. Every person that has a knowledge of the elect of God realizes it is important that he continues to press forward. He cannot endure sin nor darkness's nor things done in the shadows. The elect is so in earnest to be right for God that he burns every bridge behind him.

"Knowing this, that first there shall be a falling away."

Knowing this, that first God shall bring into His treasury the realities of the truth and put them side by side — the false, and the true, those that can be shaken in mind, and those that cannot be shaken in mind. God requires us to be so built upon the foundation of truth that we cannot be shaken in our mind; it doesn't matter what comes.

#7 Speak to The Demonic Power in the Name of Jesus

Speak to The Mountain, Believing What You Say Will Happen!

The **seventh step, principle, reality** that must be apprehended is by you speaking to the evil spirits, the affliction, sickness, disease, or ailment. Jesus Said in Mark 11: 23

Mark 11:22 And Jesus answering saith unto them, Have faith in God.23 For verily I say unto you, That whosoever shall say unto this mountain, Be thou removed, and be thou cast into the sea; and shall not doubt in his heart, but shall believe that those things which he saith shall come to pass; he shall have whatsoever he saith. 24 Therefore I say unto you, What things soever ye desire, when ye pray, believe that ye receive them, and ye shall have them.

The reality is that Jesus already purchased, paid for our deliverance and healing: physically, mentally, and emotionally when he went to Calvary. Jesus has already overcome the strong man, the demonic world in his sufferings, death, and resurrection. In the book of Jeremiah God told the young prophet that he was going to use him to change nations. He gave them a very specific word in chapter 1:

Jeremiah 1:10 See, I have this day set thee over the nations and over the kingdoms, to root out, and to pull down, and to destroy, and to throw down, to build, and to plant.

Notice the job that God had given to Jeremiah was very serious and profound. Now how in the world was Jeremiah going to be able to **root out, pull down, destroy, throw down, build, and plant** amongst these nations? We discover this answer with what God said to Jeremiah.

Jeremiah 1:9 Then the Lord put forth his hand, and touched my mouth. And the Lord said unto me, Behold, I have put my words in thy mouth.

Jeremiah 1:12 Then said the Lord unto me, Thou hast well seen: for I will hasten my word to perform it.

Jeremiah 5:14 Wherefore thus saith the Lord God of hosts, Because ye speak this word, behold, I will make my words in thy mouth fire, and this people wood, and it shall devour them.

Dr Michael H Yeager

Jeremiah 23:29 Is not my word like as a fire? saith the Lord; and like a hammer that breaketh the rock in pieces?

God has given to us the **name of Jesus**, and his **word** to **prevail, overcome, subdue every work of the enemy**. We must speak the name of Jesus and his word to that mountain, problem, adversity that is contrary to God's word and will. We must speak to the devil's, cancer, arthritis, disease, and affliction that is attacking our body, and others. Through the years as the enemy has attacked my body, I have had to rise up in faith, taking authority over the affliction and speaking the name of Jesus to the sickness, or disease, and commanding it to go in Jesus name. Christ overcame principalities and powers. **He gave unto us authority and power over every work of the enemy**. We must take that which has been given to us by Christ, and use it against the enemy.

Luke 10:19 Behold, I give unto you power to tread on serpents and scorpions, and over all the power of the enemy: and nothing shall by any means hurt you.

John 1:12 But as many as received him, to them gave he the power to become the sons of God, even to them that believe on his name:

The way the kingdom of God works is completely different than how the natural world works. Spiritual laws, principles, realities are superior to the natural laws that govern nature and humanity. God spoke through the prophet Isaiah in chapter 55 that **even as the heavens are higher than the earth, so are God's ways higher than man's ways**. As we read the word of God, we must simply receive it as it is, and never argue with the Bible. Never allow anyone to convince you that Scriptures contradict one another. Never use a Scripture to disprove another Scripture. God has never contradicted himself, and if it appears as if God is contradicting himself, it simply means you're not rightly interpreting the word. God is never wrong, he never lies, he is eternally forever the same, just, holy, and righteous. Once you receive his word, accept it as it is, then verbally you need to say to yourself **"I Believe It."** The devil will try to convince you that you're smarter than God, which is almost blasphemous in its nature. Always agree with what the word of God says even if it contradicts your experiences and even the experiences of others.

Titus 1:2 In hope of eternal life, which God, that cannot lie, promised before the world began;

Amos 3:3 Can two walk together, except they are agreed?

Once you verbally declare "**I Believe What God Says**" you are beginning to enter into the realm where all things are possible. Do not be surprised if you have to make this bold statement to yourself over 100 times a day. It will be necessary for you to say verbally to yourself that you believe God's word to overcome the spirit of unbelief, which is called the spirit of disobedience.

Ephesians 2:2 Wherein in time past ye walked according to the course of this world, according to the prince of the power of the air, the spirit that now worketh in the children of disobedience:

When I gave my heart to Jesus Christ on February 18, at about 3 o'clock in the afternoon, in 1975, I picked up my little green military New Testament Bible, declaring to myself that whatever the Bible said, I would believe it. From that time to this present age I have never argued with the word of God. Yes, I have met many people who have aggressively tried to get me to believe contrary to what Gods word says. They have tried to convince me that there is no hell, but I believe the Bible. They have tried to convince me there is no judgment to those who commit wickedness, and do not repent, but I believe the Bible. They have tried to convince me that healing is not for today, but I believe the Bible. It does not matter how I feel, how it looks, even my personal experiences. I choose to receive, believe, and act upon the truth of God's word. Jesus boldly declare: **You Have What You!**

Saying what it is you desire to come to pass before you

ever experience it, is a spiritual, and biblical truth, whether people like it or not. What you say to yourself will also determine what direction you will go in life. James likens the tongue to the **rudder** of the ship. Though the tongue is very small, even as the **rudder** of a large ship, it can turn about that mighty ship, which is driven by fierce winds.

You are Experiencing What You're Saying, & What You're Saying Is What you are Experiencing!

Do you know that the Scriptures declare that if you're born again that Jesus Christ himself lives inside of you? You might say: I just do not feel like as if Jesus lives in me! When you experience feelings that are contrary to the Bible you have one of two choices. The **first choice** is that you can disagree with God and his word, which in effect is calling God a liar. **Number two** you can say: I believe what God's word says about me, that Jesus Christ lives inside of me, and therefore I agree with God, and I do not care how I feel. How you respond to a situation when you feel something that is contrary to what God's word says will determine the ultimate outcome of your situation. Notice what the disciple of Jesus said in 1John: **You Have Overcome Them, Little Children Because Greater Is He That Is in You Than He That Is in World!** This Scripture is written to all of those who have believed, received AND accepted Jesus Christ.

It is a basic principle that if you keep saying something long enough to yourself, eventually you will end up believing it. You can either speak how you feel, the lies of the devil, your circumstances, or you can say **what God says**: to yourself about what God says about you. What you say to yourself continually you will eventually believe, and it will become your reality. This is not minded over matter, but a dynamic spiritual principle, divine laws that God has set in place. Remember When They Were Building the Tower of Babel, and They Were All Saying the Same Thing, and God Made an Amazing Statement:
Genesis 11:6 And the Lord said, Behold, the people is one, and they have all one language; and this they begin to do: and now

nothing will be restrained from them, which they have imagined to do.

A major way that I have learned to find out where I am at spiritually is by listening to what I'm saying. When the pressures of life, when afflictions come, when the enemy is attacking me, when I'm under pressure, out of my mouth will come either the truth of God's word or the lie the devil has fed me. If I find myself saying that which is contrary to God's word it simply reveals that I need to **go back to the Bible**, and put more of the word of God into my heart. It reveals to me that I have not been abiding in Christ, and in his Word the way I should.

God Created Everything by the Words of His Mouth!

What you are saying will determine where you will end up living. The place that you are now living in is because of what you have been believing, and confessing over yourself. Please understand that when I talk about confessing God's word I am not talking about you going around and **blabbing** to everybody what you believe. What you say to everybody else should be the tip of the iceberg of what you have been saying to yourself. I spend way more time speaking the word to myself, my mind, my body, my emotions, my circumstances than I do to others.

Ephesians 5:18 And be not drunk with wine, wherein is excess; but be filled with the Spirit;19 Speaking to yourselves in psalms and hymns and spiritual songs, singing and making melody in your heart to the Lord;20 Giving thanks always for all things unto God and the Father in the name of our Lord Jesus Christ;

I married my precious wife back on August 19, of 1978. After being married for some years, I found myself getting frustrated with my precious wife because she would not submit to me at times. I came up with this (what I thought was being creative) plan to get my wife to submit to me. I would simply **Fake** being upset with her when in all reality I wasn't. So the next time she did not submit to exactly what I asked her to do, I threw a

fake, miniature hissy fit. I acted like I was mad, and upset with her, acting angry. In all reality, I was not angry, but I told her I was, and how I felt about what she did by disobeying me. The next time she did not submit to me, I followed the same routine but with a little bit more emphasis, telling her how upset I was with her. This continued for some weeks when all of a sudden to my **horror** I found myself No Longer **Faking** my anger fits, but I was beginning to be totally engulfed with anger and rage at her for not submitting.

Without knowing it, I had opened the door to a satanic influence. I went to prayer over it asking God what happened? He simply told me that I got what I was confessing. Now, in all sincerity, I did not want to be angry and upset with my precious wife. When the Lord revealed this to me, and what I had done, I quickly repented to him, and then I went to my wife, confessing to her what I had been doing, and the results of that manipulation. I repented, asking her to forgive me. Praise God; I was delivered!

Proverbs 18:21 Death and life are in the power of the tongue: and they that love it shall eat the fruit thereof.

---

1 John 5:4 For whatsoever is born of God overcometh the world: and this is the victory that overcometh the world, even our faith. 5 Who is he that overcometh the world, but he that believeth that Jesus is the Son of God?

In the book of Revelation over and over, it declares that we must overcome. Those who overcome will be clothed in white raiment, and their names will be written down on white stones that no man knows but God himself. **Jesus** has already overcome all principalities and powers. He said to his disciples in Matthew:

Behold all authority has been given to me in heaven & in the earth, go therefore in to the entire world and preach the gospel to every creature.

For whatsoever is born of God, overcomes the world! John is very specific about who overcomes. This is John who was the beloved of **Jesus**, the one who laid his head on the chest of **Jesus** at the last meal. He was the only Apostle who was there at the cross when **Christ** suffered and died. He was the first of the 11 apostles who arrived at the tomb on resurrection morning. John boldly declared that the victory that overcomes the world is **faith** in **Jesus Christ**. Faith is the declaration of trust, reliance, and dependence upon **Christ**. To overcome means to conquer, triumph, prevail, subdue and have victory. Hebrews chapter 11 reveals to us 50 major events that were accomplished by faith in **Jesus Christ**.

What's amazing is that if you look up the word faith in the four Gospels, it appears many times in Matthew, Mark, and Luke, but in the gospel of John the word faith does not appear even one time. Instead, we see the emphasis on the word **believe**! Believe and faith are the same, but the word to **believe** has a deeper and more personal connotation to it than the word faith. It brings to mind a much more intimate relationship.

1 John 5:1 Whosoever believeth that Jesus is the Christ is born of God: and every one that loveth him that begat loveth him also that is begotten of him. 2 By this we know that we love the children of God when we love God, and keep his commandments. 3 For this is the love of God, that we keep his commandments: and his commandments are not grievous.

In verse three it declares that we keep his commandments. This is a faith that works by love. This is the declaration of our faith in **Jesus Christ**. In one situation **Jesus** asked the multitudes: *why do you call me, Lord, Lord, and do not the things I say?* In another situation, he said: *who is my mother brother and sister, but they that do the will of my Father which is in heaven!*

We are called to keep the commandments of **Christ** and **to do them,** by doing the **word of God,** you will **experience deliverance** and **healing**! James declares that faith without works is dead. What we do with our time, resources, energy, mind, and body reveals who we are, because what you love reveals who you are, and that which you love possesses you. **Jesus** declared: *for where your heart is there your treasuries is also*. There is a song I love to sing that declares: *I love to praise him!* There are many Scriptures that declare the love that God's people have for his word.

Jeremiah 15:16 Thy words were found, and I did eat them; and thy word was unto me the joy and rejoicing of mine heart: for I am called by thy name, O Lord God of hosts.

Psalm 119:47 And I will delight myself in thy commandments, which I have loved.

Psalm 1:2 But his delight is in the law of the Lord, and in his law doth he meditate day and night.

James 4:17 Therefore to him that knoweth to do good, and doeth it not, to him it is sin.

1Corinthians 11:3 But I fear, lest by any means, as the serpent beguiled Eve through his subtilty, so your minds should be corrupted from the simplicity that is in Christ.

Thank the **Father** that **Jesus** did not fail to obey the will of the Father by Faith. Because of his obedience even to death upon the cross, the **Father** has highly exalted him, and given him a name that is above every name!

There are many that call themselves believers, but their religion is in vain because they are not exercising any faith when it comes to obeying the word, the will, the plans, and the purposes of God. This is extremely displeasing to our heavenly **Father**. When **Jesus** himself returns with the angelic host, he will separate the sheep from the goats. And he will take vengeance on them that have not obeyed the gospel.

2 Thessalonians 1:8 in flaming fire taking vengeance on them that know not God, and that obey not the gospel of our Lord Jesus Christ:

Where Faith Is Alive - The Flesh Will Die!

Jesus declared heaven and earth shall pass away, but my words will never pass away. Every promise, provision, and blessing that **Christ** spoke of his church can be trusted. Now on the other side of the coin I can also guarantee that every warning he spoke will come to pass upon those who will not exercise faith to hear and obey.

Matthew 7:21 Not every one that saith unto me, Lord, Lord, shall enter into the kingdom of heaven; but he that doeth the will of my Father which is in heaven. 22 Many will say to me in that day, Lord, Lord, have we not prophesied in thy name? And in thy name have cast out devils? and in thy name done many wonderful works? 23 And then will I profess unto them, I never knew you: depart from me, ye that work iniquity.

#8 You Have Need of Patience

The **eighth step, truth, reality** in casting out Devils is **Patience**! It is very difficult for many people to wait patiently for the manifestation of the deliverance. One of the major problems is that they associate deliverance with the manifestation. For another word they do not believe that they or the person they're ministering to is delivered until they feel it, see it, and experience it. Here is an amazing experience that **Smith Wigglesworth** had in casting out a devil.

Demon Possessed Man Healed

(Wiggelsworth) I was one time asked to go to Weston-super-mare, a seaside resort in the West of England. I learned from a telegram that a man had lost his reason and had become a raving maniac, and they wanted me to go to pray for him. I arrived at the place, and the wife said to me, "Will you sleep with my husband?" I agreed, and in the middle of the night, an evil power laid hold of him. It was awful. I put my hand on his head, and his hair was like a lot of sticks. God gave deliverance-a temporary deliverance. At 6 o'clock the next morning, I felt that it was necessary that I should get out of the house for a short time.

The man saw me going and cried out, "If you leave me, there is no hope." But I felt that I had to go. As I went out, I saw a woman with a Salvation Army bonnet on, and I knew that she was going to their 7 o'clock prayer meeting. I said to the Captain who was in charge of the meeting, when I saw he was about to give out a hymn, "Captain, don't sing. Let's get to prayer." He agreed, and I prayed my heart out, and then I grabbed my hat and rushed out of the hall. They all thought they had a madman in their prayer meeting that morning.

I saw the man I had spent the night with, rushing down toward the sea, without a particle of clothing on, about to drown himself. I cried, **"In the name of Jesus, come out of him!"** The man fell full length on the ground, and that evil power went out of him never to return. His wife came rushing after him, and the husband was restored to her in a perfect mental condition.

There are evil powers, but Jesus is greater than all evil powers. There are tremendous diseases, but Jesus is a healer. There is no case too hard for Him. The Lion of Judah shall break every chain. He came to relieve the oppressed and to set the captive free. He came to bring redemption, to make us as perfect as the man was before the fall.

People want to know how to be kept by the power of God.

Every position of grace into which you are led-forgiveness, healing, deliverance of any kind, will be contested by Satan. He will contend for your body. When you are saved, Satan will come round and say, "See, you are not saved." The devil is a liar. If he says you are not saved, it is a sure sign that you are.

Patience is directly connected to our faith and that which we are hoping, believing for. In Hebrews 10:38 emphasizes the importance of enduring and having patience.

Hebrews 10:36 For ye have need of patience, that, after ye have done the will of God, ye might receive the promise.

Having patience is a long-distance runner. In high school, I used to run cross-country track. A sprinter and a long-distance runner are two different things. A sprinter may run 100 yards, whereas a long-distance runner will have to run many miles. Speed is necessary for a sprinter to win a race. Cross country runners not only need speed, but they need endurance. In the thesaurus the **Synonyms** for endurance are:

abidance, ceaselessness, continuance, continuity, continuousness, durability, duration, continuation, persistence, subsistence

*20. Hindu Girl Delivered of demons. (2011)

My son and I were ministering in a little country in South America called Suriname. While in this country we were able to get a close look at a religion called Hinduism. I had never realized how demonic this religion was and is. Their temples are filled with nothing but statues and pictures of gods that look just like demons. There is no doubt whatsoever in my heart or mind that they are demons sent to deceive the masses. Dealing with these demons did not concern me (though I had been warned ahead of time) in the least, having dealt with demonic powers, and demon possessed people from my early days with the Lord.

Now, when I am in other countries sharing the gospel, there is one thing I hate, and that is to sit around and do nothing. I am always looking for opportunities even when there are no meetings taking place. We were going to be speaking in a poverty-stricken part of Suriname that night in a church that they were still constructing. All of the frameworks had been laid for this small facility, including the concrete floor, and the steel sheeting on the roof. We had arrived in the early afternoon for that evening's meeting. I suggested to the pastor that we should visit people, possibly from door to door in this area. Many of the houses we visited (according to our standards) were more like shacks and sheds then livable accommodations. As we went from house to house, we would knock on the door, and wait for a response. The pastor would introduce who we were, invite them to the meeting, and then try to share some of the gospel.

About halfway through the morning, into the early afternoon, we came to one particular house. A young lady who seemed to be dressed in Hindu garb came to the door. She stepped out of her house and closed the door behind her as the pastor began to speak to her. She seemed to be a young lady in her early 20s, with sunken eyes, and a very thin face, and a visible oppression upon her. As I began to share the gospel with her (the pastor interpreting) demonic spirits manifested themselves. Her eyes rolled up in her head, and she began to go into the contortions of a seizure. She fell to the ground and began to squirm in a very torturous fashion. Now, you would think that I would be instantly alarmed and upset in this situation, but that was not the case.

I have been in similar situations when demons have manifested themselves. When this happens you better make sure that you're walking with God, and you know the voice of the spirit. As this young lady fell to the ground in contortions, my son, and myself, including the pastor all stepped a little bit away from her. Immediately the pastor got excited, more like upset. He began to try to cast the devil out of her right away with loud and authoritative words. This went on for probably about five minutes as he was commanding the demons to come out in his language.

I finally touched him on the shoulder getting his attention, putting my finger to my lips in a fashion of saying, be quiet. With over 40 years of experience, I have discovered that you do not have to yell and scream at Devils, and it does not take a long time to cast them out.

That is if you are submitted to God, following Jesus, living a holy life, then, and only then will you have the authority that the enemy must submit to.

When the pastor stopped, I simply pointed my finger at the young lady and said in a quiet voice, but with authority: **you lying devil's, in the Name of Jesus Christ of Nazareth come out of her NOW!** After I spoke **One Time**, I simply stepped back and stood there looking at the young lady. The seizure and contortions continued, even getting worse, but it did not move me. I knew the demons had to leave. These contortions and squirming's continued for about three or four minutes longer. The pastor was looking at me as if I had lost my mind.

All of a sudden I saw by the Spirit of God that the demons had left her. The countenance on her face which had been so hard twisted and tormented, instantly changed. A wonderful softness, innocence came upon her. There was a divine glow that overtook her face. Tears began to roll down her cheeks, and at the same time, they began to roll down my cheeks. It was so wonderful and moving to see this young lady delivered from these demonic spirits of Hinduism. I cannot describe to you the great joy that came upon me at that moment when I saw her set free.

Mark 9:25 When Jesus saw that the people came running together, he rebuked the foul spirit, saying unto him, Thou dumb and deaf spirit, I charge thee, come out of him, and enter no more into him.26 And the spirit cried, and rent him sore, and came out of him: and he was as one dead; insomuch that many said, He is dead.27 But Jesus took him by the hand, and lifted him up; and he arose.

Many so-called ministers who boldly declare that they have deliverance ministries spend way too much time glorifying the devil. I am convinced that they are sincere in their beliefs, but in the way, they deal with demonic powers it is obvious they have not studied the four Gospels. My training in casting out Devils was given to me by the Holy Spirit and by looking at the ministry of Jesus Christ. He never spent hours on and trying to get the devil is to come out of people. He simply spoke with authority, compassion, faith, and power to those evil spirits.

He told them to shut up, and to come out!

This is exactly how I have been doing it for over 40 years. The results I get are completely dependent upon where I am at spiritually with Christ. If I am walking in harmony with God, obedience, holiness, in faith, then the results are instantaneous and always complete.

Now I had the wonderful opportunity to lead this Hindu girl to Christ. That night she was in our service praising and worshiping God with the glory of the Lord upon her. About a year later we were back once again ministering in this church, and this young lady was still there worshiping Christ with the presence of God upon her life. Jesus had set her free from the demonic spirits of Hinduism!

There are many scriptures in the Bible that deals with the subject of patience and endurance when it comes to the believer and his faith. As we are believing God that **We People Are Delivered,** we will have need of patience and endurance.

Matthew 24:13 But he that shall endure unto the end, the same shall be saved.

Mark 4:17 And have no root in themselves, and so endure but for a time: afterward, when affliction or persecution ariseth for the word's sake, immediately they are offended.

1 Corinthians 13:7 Beareth all things, believeth all things, hopeth all things, endureth all things.

2 Timothy 2:3 Thou therefore endure hardness, as a good soldier of Jesus Christ.

2 Timothy 4:5 But watch thou in all things, endure afflictions, do the work of an evangelist, make full proof of thy ministry.

Hebrews 6:15 And so, after he had patiently endured, he obtained the promise.

In the book of James, the brother of Jesus gives to us wonderful insights on the importance of patience. Many believers have the wrong concept in thinking that the minute they prayed that if they are in faith, they should have an immediate manifestation of their healing or deliverance. The Bible says that they that believe shall lay their hands on the sick, and **they shall recover**. Please notice the word **recover**. It implies a length of time involved in the manifestation or the evidence of the healing. Yes, I love it when I pray for someone, or myself, and see instantaneous results. If I do not see instantaneous results, this does not mean that I am not healed, or the person I prayed for is not healed or delivered. The Scripture says that **they shall recover**.

Many times when I pray for people, I will encourage them to go ahead and check to see if there is any change in their body whatsoever. Most times there will be a little bit of a change in their physical condition. When Peter prayed for the man at the gate beautiful, the Bible says he received strength in his ankle bones.

Acts 3:5 And he gave heed unto them, expecting to receive something of them.6 Then Peter said, Silver and gold have I none; but such as I have give I thee: In the name of Jesus Christ of Nazareth rise up and walk.7 And he took him by the right hand, and lifted him up: and immediately his feet and ankle bones received strength.

It was after Peter prayed that this crippled man received a little bit of strength in his ankle bones. This man **immediately acted upon that little bit of a manifestation,** and he began to leap and dance. He acted upon that little bit of a manifestation in his body without being told to! His actions were a manifestation of his faith.

Many times when I have prayed for people with bad backs immediately after I pray, I tell them to reach for their toes with their fingertips. At their first stretch, most of them can barely bend over. I tell them to reach once again with their fingers for their toes. The second time they can go about half way. I tell them once again to reach further for their toes with their fingertips. By the third time that they stretch for their toes, acting upon my instructions, many of them see the manifestation of their healing. We must act upon that which we have spoken of faith over our bodies. If you do not see instantaneous results, you must never let go of the fact that by his stripes **You Were Healed!**

James 1:3 Knowing this, that the trying of your faith worketh patience'

James 1:4 But let patience have her perfect work, that ye may be perfect and entire, wanting nothing.

James 5:10 Take, my brethren, the prophets, who have spoken in the name of the Lord, for an example of suffering affliction, and of patience.:11 Behold, we count them happy which endure. Ye have heard of the patience of Job, and have seen the end of the Lord; that the Lord is very pitiful, and of tender mercy.

When I Take a Hold of the Will of God, specifically when it comes to my Healing, I am Speaking the Word, I'm Thanking God, I'm Laughing at the Devil, and during This Time of Patience, I keep an attitude of FAITH! **I Am Thanking God That His Word Is Real, and I'm Laughing at the Devil**. It is like starting a fire in your fireplace. Once you have a flame burning in the wood stove, you keep feeding the fire fuel until it is a raging, hot, enduring flame. If you are using a wood fire in your house to keep your house warm you must naturally be putting wood in the fire all through the day, and through the long cold night so that the fire will not go out. It is the same with receiving your healing. You must maintain a constant faith by acting upon the word until you see the manifestation.

Romans 8:24 For we are saved by hope: but hope that is seen is not hope: for what a man seeth, why doth he yet hope for? :25 But if we hope for that we see not, then do we with patience wait for it.

Let Me Go over These **8 Points** once again very quickly.

Number 1- You Must Exalt Jesus Christ above all else. He is GOD!

Number 2- You must enter into the Arena of Faith in CHRIST. In His Name is all Authority and Power!

Number 3 - Eat and Drink the Word of God Night and Day.

Number 4 - You Must Be Extremely Serious about setting people Free.

Number 5 Never Exalt the devil or the Afflictions.

Number 6 - - Examine Your Heart and Simply Confess Your Sins. Repent and Turn Away from Them, Believing God to Get Victory over them.

Number 7- Speak to the evil spirits, Knowing in your Heart that they have to obey you.

Number 8 - You Have Need of Patience That after You Have Done the Will of God You May Receive the Promise!

CHAPTER TEN

HOW THE ENEMY IS CONSTANTLY ATTACKING

THIS IS VERY SERIOUS BUSINESS, AND WE BETTER TREAT AS SUCH. WHENEVER YOU BEGIN TO CAST OUT DEVILS, AND OPERATE IN THE AUTHORITY, AND THE POWER THAT CHRIST HAS GIVEN TO US, THE ENEMY IS SURE TO SHOW UP. IN THIS CHAPTER I RELATE STORIES OF HOW THROUGH THE YEARS, THE ENEMY HAS TRY TO DESTROY MYSELF, MY FAMILY, AND THOSE I LOVE AND KNOW.

*21. Stop, Stop, Stop (downtown DC) 2013

The devil is always working overtime to kill us by whatever means he has available, whether sickness, accidents, crime, war, or by multitudes of other attacks! Here is a good example.

My sons Daniel's wife to be (Catherine Yu Lee) was flying in from California in the month of February. She was coming to attend a woman's conference that the ladies of our church were attending in West Lafayette Indiana. We were going to have to pick her up at Dulles International Airport later in the evening. During this time I was going through a terrible attack by the devil with horrible physical afflictions. My equilibrium was completely haywire, and everything was spinning, plus some type of flu had hit my stomach, and I was running a high fever, with chills. Normally I would've simply driven with my wife to pick Catherine up, but I was in no physical condition to drive or to go along with them.

It was agreed upon that my wife and my son Daniel would go pick up Catherine at the right time. As I was lying in bed, miserable as all get out, running a high fever, with chills racking my body, an urgency came upon me in my heart as they were getting ready to leave. Now it would make no sense in the natural to go along with them seeing that I was sick, but when I receive a quickening of the Lord like this, I do not argue with God. My wife and son were just walking out the door to leave when I called out from our bedroom for my wife. She came to see what I wanted, and I told her that I needed to go with them to the airport to pick up Catherine. She, of course, tried to encourage me to stay home and to rest. I simply told her I needed to go with them. I wrapped myself in the back seat of my wife's Toyota Prius with a bunch of blankets, and I laid down for the journey.

It was not long before I fell into a deep sleep. It turns out that about two hours later as my wife and son were driving through DC, they had become lost. They were total, completely, and utterly lost, and confused where they were at. Now as I'm sleeping soundly in the backseat of the car, I heard the voice of God speak to me almost audibly. In bold, strong words, I heard the Lord say: Wake up Now! The minute I heard the Lord say this, I immediately snapped out of this deep sleep. I sat up in the back seat of the Toyota Prius completely awake and clear minded. I stuck my head between my wife and my son looking out the front window of the car. What I saw was heavy traffic all around us, and we were headed towards a signal light about 50 feet ahead that had just turned yellow. My wife was going too fast, and I could see that she was not going to stop.

The light turned red, but she just kept going talking to Daniel as she went along. I said to her out loud: Stop! She did not seem to hear a word I said. Again I said to her: stop as she went through the red light. Now heavy traffic was headed towards us from the left and the right side. The third time I said with the voice of authority: Kathy **STOP NOW**! Finally, something registered in her mind, and she slammed on the brakes. Here we were stuck in the middle of the intersection with traffic headed towards us on both sides. I told her to put the car in reverse and to back up to the signal light. Thank God she complied with me without us having a major accident. I am telling you that it was an absolute miracle that we did not get slammed by the vehicles on the left side and the right side of the car.

I could tell that a spirit of confusion had completely engulfed my wife and son because they were in heavy traffic, and they had gotten lost. I told her to put the car in park. Once the car was stopped at the traffic light, I jumped out of the vehicle, opened up her car door, and told her to let me take over driving. She complied with my directions. Once the light turned green, we were on our way once again, thankfully getting to the airport, and picking up Catherine.

*22. Colon Cancer will not kill me!

I began to experience some very disturbing symptoms in my body. I will not go into all the details, but there were approximately nine different physical symptoms. One of the symptoms was almost every time I had a bowel movement; it looked as if all my innards were coming out. During this three month period, I was so sick sometimes that I thought that I was going to die at any moment. My normal course of action is that the minute my body begins to manifest any sickness or disease, I immediately command it to go in the Name of Jesus Christ of Nazareth!

But these symptoms simply refuse to leave. I made a list of everything that was happening in my body and then I looked these symptoms up on the internet. Every one of them pointed to colon cancer. I had gone through a similar fight of faith some years previously, with what seemed to be prostate cancer. Once again, I took hold of the Word of God. I boldly declared to the devil, myself and the spiritual world that I would live and not die. I cried out to Jesus for His mercy and His grace in the midst of this fight of faith. This fight was almost overwhelming and excruciating at times!

For these three months, I continued with this fight. I spoke to the symptoms commanding them to go. I kept praising, thanking and worshiping God that I was healed; no ifs, ands or buts. I declared boldly that the devil is a liar. For three months every day, all day at times, declaring what God said about me. I did not invite anybody else to stand with me in this fight of faith. Most people, if they would have known what I was going through, would have pronounced me dead and gone. Believe it or not, they are people who call themselves Christians who would've rejoiced in my death. Yes, they would've been telling people to pray, but there would have been more negative comments than the reality of God's Word.

By His stripes, we were healed! If I were healed, then I was healed, if I was healed than I am healed and if I am healed then I is healed! For three long months I stood and fought by faith. Many nights and days walking the floor of our church sanctuary praising God that I was healed, resisting the spirit of fear. One day I woke up and all of the symptoms had disappeared, praise God. And they have never come back. Thank you Jesus!!

*23. A Prophetic Divine Warning!

I had a dream last night about 3 o'clock in the morning. My daughter and I were walking down a beautiful path through a forest on a path that we knew would take us home. On the right side of us were many beautiful pine trees. It was an amazing and beautiful midday walk through the Forrest. Ahead of us, off to the right, I saw an extremely large and beautiful pine tree. At the bottom of this pine tree, there was a large perfectly formed round dirt hole. As we were walking towards this tree, I saw a mother and her son coming from the opposite direction. Her son was approximately eight years old. About 30 feet away from this large pine tree, coming up out of this dirt hole popped the head and half of the body of a very large, beautiful red tailed fox.

This fox seemed to be a little bit larger than most foxes that I have personally seen in my life. This foxes coat glistened in the beautiful sun, and it had a brilliant white streak running down the front of its chest. This fox was so beautiful that it made you want to run to it, hold it to your chest, and pet it. Now this fox seemed to be extremely friendly, almost begging for attention, and as it came up out of the hole, it laid down on the left side on the fresh brown dirt. The little boy saw this fox with his mother and ran towards this beautiful big fox. Now this little boy had a wonderfully big and excited smile on his face. His mother was watching this unfold, and seemed to be in complete approval of his actions, she also a large smile on her face.

I and my daughter also felt within us a desire to go and hold this large beautiful red tail fox, which was fluffy and adorable, almost Walt Disney adorable in its character. My daughter and I unknowingly increase our walk to get to this Fox for we could crawl into its hole with it, and hold it. In the midst of our excitement, red lights began to go off in my heart. A thought came to my mind: what is a fox doing, coming out of its hole at this time of day. Foxes normally are night time creatures,(nocturnal animals) and not daytime wanderers. Instantly I knew what was going on. This was not a friendly fox, but a very sick fox, which had rabies. Fear flooded my whole body.

Instantly I began to cry out to this boy and mother to stay away from this sick rabid Fox, but it was too late. The boy had already fallen into the hole with this fox. As it began to attack the boy, I saw the other side of its face. The gums were pulled back, with terrible red blood and pussy teeth protruding from the right side of us pulled back gums. It was a terrible sight to behold. I told my daughter to run for safety, not wanting this fox to attack her. Personally, I began to run towards this little boy, but already knowing that it was already too late to help him. As I ran towards this little boy who was being attacked by the Fox in the hole, I had no idea what I could do to rescue him.

At this very moment in this part of the dream, I woke up praying with deep urgency in my heart. It was about 4 o'clock, and I knew instantly in my heart the understanding and the interpretation of this dream. Many people in the body of Christ are being deceived into believing, embracing and partaking of that which seems to be harmless and beautiful, but in reality, it is like a rabid fox. The devil has come to us as an angel of light through many different avenues which seem to be harmless, but in all reality are extremely deadly and destructive to our well-being. Not only have our children embraced that which is demonic and destructive, but we as parents have encouraged them, approved, and are involved with them in these activities. May God have mercy on us and deliver us from all of these lies.

*24. You're a dead man (1981)

I heard the audible voice of God say, "You're a Dead Man!"

I was driving into Mount Union, Pennsylvania with my wife to do some grocery shopping. I was driving a sports Ford Granada with a 302 Engine. The urge came to me to put the pedal to the metal and let it roar. The Lord had already delivered me from speeding years ago, but at that moment it was as if a devil took hold of me. I willingly gave in to this urge as I mashed down on the gas pedal and began to increase my speed. Yes, I knew better, but I caved and gave into temptation. My wife looked over at me just shaking her head. (Someone else was watching our newborn son Michael so he was not with us.)

I ended up accelerating to over 80 miles per hour. Kathleen was praying out loud that if we had an accident, she would not be hurt because of my stupidity and then she began to pray faster in the spirit. I was coming around the corner on Route 747 right before you entered into the Mount Union when I heard the audible voice of God say to me, **"You are a Dead Man!"** Instantly the fear of the Lord hit me like a sledgehammer. The fear of God went right to the very marrow of my bones. I saw a stop sign ahead of me to the left and the right. At that very moment, I slammed on the brakes of my car, instantly slowing down.

A flash of white zipped past my left. I mean right then and there I saw a totally white, souped-up Dodge Charger come speeding through the stop sign from the left. He ran the stop sign without stopping or slowing up in the least. I mean he had the pedal to the metal. I'm convinced he must've been going over 80 miles an hour. If I had not slammed on my brakes exactly when I heard the audible voice of God, his car would have slammed right into my driver's side door. There is no doubt in my mind or my heart that I would have been instantly killed. Thank God for his long-suffering and mercy.

1 Peter 5:8 Be sober, be vigilant; because your adversary the devil, as a roaring lion, walketh about, seeking whom he may devour:9 Whom resist stedfast in the faith, knowing that the same afflictions are accomplished in your brethren that are in the world. 1 Peter 5:8-9 (KJV)

*25. My Neck Was in the Guillotine!

I had been pastoring in Gettysburg, Pennsylvania for approximately three years (1986). To be honest with you, if I had my preferences as to where to pastor, it would've never been here in Gettysburg. Even statistically, there are many places which are much more open to the things of God than this religious, stiff-necked, hard to deal with the area. Gettysburg has come to be known as the ghost capital of America because of their ghost walks, spiritual séances, and fortune-telling. I am not talking about the Holy Ghost, either. Nor does this include all of the the religious spirits that are in the area, evidenced by their cold, dead seminaries and religious colleges. I know that there are many who think that where they are laboring is extremely difficult. They may very well be right. For over 30 years, my family and I have labored in this field, seeing very little results, and yet when I go to other areas, God truly shows up. Please don't misunderstand me, yes we have had many moves of God, many healed, many signs and wonders, and yet seen very little enduring fruit. People get healed, delivered, set free and then leave to go to some lukewarm, seeker-friendly atmosphere. You might ask, "Why are you here then?" Because this is where God has called us to labor in His vineyard.

Back to my story: So, I had been pastoring for about three years in this area, when one night I went to sleep as I normally did. This time; however, I had a very frightening and real dream. This dream was not just a figment of my imagination or some kind of stomach disorder caused by something disagreeable that I ate.

In this dream, I was confronted by one of the major ruling spiritual principalities and powers in this area. Here I was sleeping soundly, when suddenly in this dream, I was in a very large mansion. I could tell that it was a historical mansion built in the style of the late 1800s. I found myself in a very large dining room with fancy woodwork, chairs, and other furniture that one would expect in a very wealthy man's house. I could tell that I was on the west side of the house looking towards the east when a young lady came walking through a set of very fancy, wooden, double doors. Right away I could tell that there was something wrong with this picture and felt in my heart that I was in great danger, so I began to look around for a way of escape. Right behind me was a single, wooden door that exited the dining room. I immediately ran for this door, entering into a large kitchen with cooking equipment. The floor of this room was made up of large white and black tiles with tables aligned from east to west in a long row used for food preparation. To my right were sinks with old-style faucets and other cooking equipment. To my left were cabinets, meat hooks, large cooking pots and kitchen supplies.

What immediately caught my attention though was that right in front of me, approximately 20 feet away, was the most frighteningly tall and skinny man that I had ever seen. I knew in my heart right away that this was a ruling principality and power in this geographical area. He had on a three-piece suit, dark in color, with some kind of checkered shirt covered by a leather vest. He was also wearing an old-style bow tie that was common in the 1800s. His face was long, ugly and skinny, yet highly educated and intelligent. Evil radiated from him almost like an invisible aroma that filled the air with a terrible, wicked stench. He was smiling at me with a very large, grotesque grin, almost like the Joker from the Batman genre. Immediately fear, overwhelming fear filled my heart. I had just run from the dining room, escaping the dangerous young lady. Now, as I looked upon this evil spirit, I completely forgot about the young lady in the other room. My instincts were to flee. I turned around to go back through the door I had just come through to escape this wicked, sophisticated, evil and twisted demon.

As I ran back into the dining room, the young lady was still standing there, but now she had taken off her top blouse and was standing there with just a black bra on in a very enticing way. When I saw her, I was hit with a double dose of fear. Sweat began to bead upon my forehead causing me to spin around and head back to the kitchen from which I came. Turning, I confronted the tall, skinny, sophisticated demon as he is coming through the kitchen door. He was laughing uncontrollably, looking directly at me. I was stuck right in the middle between this devil and the partly undressed demoness.

At that very moment, I woke up sitting up in my bed, shivering and shaking with fear and apprehension. This dream began to torment me for some months, not fully comprehending what it could mean until it finally dissipated into my unconsciousness. I never did tell my wife about this particular dream because it was so frightening and demonic. I did not want to tell anybody about it since I didn't understand what it meant.

About five years had come and gone since I had had this frightening and terrible dream. In the interim, our new church building had been completed. Not only had we built a new church but a new parsonage as well, where my family and I were living. My wife and I had three sons and one daughter. Everything was so hectic in our house that it was necessary for us to find someone to stay with us to help with the children. My sister Deborah had been doing this, but she had moved away. We took in an ordinary, young lady who attended our church to help with the children, laundry, and other family activities. Everything seemed to be going along just fine, but there was an undercurrent that began to erode away slowly our family unity.

This young lady began to become a part of our family, laughing and joking, all of us teasing one another. Unbeknownst to me, things began to happen slowly but surely like a frog being slow-boiled. I began to have wrong thoughts and desires creep into my mind. In the beginning, I cast them down, taking authority over them. We had an above ground swimming pool in the backyard of our parsonage where my wife, this young lady and my children would swim. We would all end up laughing together, splashing and just acting silly. I began to find myself getting carried away with acting like an idiot. My wife began to notice this and tried to talk to me about the fact that I was a little bit too friendly. Of course, I vehemently denied this, deceiving myself. I was headed for a major downfall, and the devil was laughing all the way. It finally came to the point where something was about to happen that would destroy myself, my family, the church and everything that God had blessed me with if God did not divinely intervene. The good news is that many times the devil overplays his hand.

I went to bed one night as I normally did, falling into a very deep, deep sleep when, out of the blue, I was back in the very same dream from five years before, back in the very house where I had been previously. Once again, I was in the dining room with the same scenario. There were the young lady and the other demon laughing at me, over and over. Once again in this dream, my heart filled with fear, my mind, and my soul became overwhelmed with great dread, when suddenly, I heard the voice of God speak to me from heaven: "This is that which you saw in the dream." Immediately, I knew in my heart what was going on in this dream. Up to this moment, I was utterly and completely ignorant of the trap that the devil had set for my destruction. My head was already in the guillotine with the blade ready to drop, and I did not even know it.

I woke up weeping and crying, broken in my heart over the lust that had begun to consume me. I woke up my wife crying and began to confess to her the dream that I previously had five years before. Then I told her what had been going on in my mind towards this young lady, confessing that my wife was right all along and that it was true that lust had become the focus of my heart. (Thank God nothing ever did happen). I wept, and I cried, then I repented. My wife held me, forgiving me for everything. We prayed together, crying out to Jesus for help, thanking Him for His mercy and His grace. God had rescued me once again from my spiritual blindness and fleshly lusts. Thank God for His mercy and the loving-kindness and forgiveness displayed to us by the Great Shepherd of the sheep, our Savior and Messiah, Jesus Christ!

2 Timothy 2:25-26 in meekness instructing those that oppose themselves; if God peradventure will give them repentance to the acknowledging of the truth; 26 and that they may recover themselves out of the snare of the devil, who are taken captive by him at his will.

*26.The Violent Take It By FORCE!
(2013)

I was lying in bed back in 2013 when I heard the audible voice of God, and he said to me: the violent take it by force! For a while now this has been marinating in my soul. Sometimes when God speaks to me, it takes time for it to become a reality. It could be four years later or maybe decades as the spirit of God will be at work on my inside. You could say that it is like a woman when she gets pregnant, life is growing inside of her womb. Even so, faith begins as a seed, and must grow within us, in our hearts. We have a lot to do with that faith growing, expanding, enlarging and becoming mature.

Please understand everybody has faith, everybody was born with a measure, a proportion of faith. When Jesus shared the parables about the ten virgins who were asleep, they all woke up when the trumpet sounded, but Jesus said there were five foolish and five wise. The Five that were wise had enough oil to take them to the arrival of their husband to be. I believe that the oil that Jesus was speaking about is the oil of faith; I believe it's faith in God and Jesus Christ.

People who do not have sufficient faith in this time period are going to have it rough. They're going to try to find somebody that has faith, but it will be too late. Then there are those who have faith which has been in hibernation. Faith can be lying dormant inside of you for many years, and then all of a sudden something supernatural happens, and it begins to come forth like a bear coming out of hibernation!

*27. Preachers used of the devil.

I had a well-known lady who spoke here one time at a women's conference. I invited her, because I had listened to some of her messages someone gave me, and they were powerful and wonderful. When she spoke at our conference, her messages were marvelous, filled with wisdom and revelation. Now after one of the meetings, all of the speakers, including myself and my wife went out to eat. Something extremely shocking and disheartening happened as we were sitting there around the table eating and listening to her speak.

As this lady began to open her mouth at the table what came out of her mouth was terrible. I never heard such garbage, gossip and complaining come out of one person's mouth in such a short period. In the pulpit, as she ministered the word of God, truth and revelation came forth, but in her private life what came out of her mouth was terrible.

I ran into another similar situation some years ago. There was a young man that the Lord had me help, giving him the opportunity to speak for the first time in his life in our pulpit. I knew by the spirit of the Lord when I met him that he was called to preach, and to teach the word of God, even though I had never heard him speak. From the very moment he began to speak, it became obvious to everyone that heard him that the spirit of the Lord was calling him to preach. Now, there was only one MAJOR issue that I could see that would destroy every endeavor that he would ever try to accomplish for Christ; it was the fact that he was extremely critical and faultfinding of almost everybody he knew. I constantly encouraged him not to be finding fault with others, but to no avail.

Even those he called his closest friends, relatives, and even his wife, behind their backs he would be constantly finding fault, and speak negatively about them. Every time he would say something negative about a person, I would try to come back with something positive about the person. Now this was a generational curse that was passed on from his mother, and from his grandmother, and who knows how many other generations.

This young man had no concept of respecting those in authority because he had been raised from a child by those who had no respect for authority. For two years, I prayed daily for him, and his family members that they would be delivered from this satanic attitude. (I still continue to pray) While my wife and I were gone to another country, that spirit rose up in him, and he began to speak to the congregation evil and slanderous words about myself, and my family. When we arrived back from our journey overseas, people who had been with us for years were now gone. I'm not speaking evil of this particular person, just the fact that we need to walk tenderly and softly before the Lord. We will be judged by the same judgment that we judge others with. We need to deal with these generational curses that are so deeply rooted in our mind and our heart, that without Christ we will never be delivered and set free from. God can use us in such wonderful ways as we are ministering the Word, by the Holy Spirit, and yet the enemy can use us in such devastating ways out of the pulpit.

*28. Deaf man's ear healed! (2014)

I rent rooms to single men at a boarding house. A brand-new tenant moved in to one of the rooms. Because it was the Fourth of July, I could not get together with him until right away. He texts me that night with an ongoing conversation, informing me that he had to get free from a demonic ENTITY! He asked if I could help him with this situation. As far as I know, he did not know that I was a minister. I asked him if he had taken the name of Jesus Christ to this ENTITY (not knowing whether he believed in Christ)? He responded by texting that in no way would he ever use that name because he was too afraid to.

The next morning at approximately 9 o'clock I arrived at the house to meet him, and his name was Todd. He was a man about my age and my height, who turns out to be a construction worker, who builds houses. I asked him to tell me his story; that is about this entity. He informed me that his grandmother was involved in some Satanic activity, and at the age of nine, these demonic powers began to oppress him, literally physically shoving him many times into the walls. As a young man, he eventually became an alcoholic because he was using the alcohol to try to suppress these attacks. Actually, the opposite of what he wanted happened, and instead of getting better he just got worse and eventually ending up in trouble.

He was now approximately 58 years old, and it had been going on for almost 50 years. He had tried to get relief, but nothing seemed to help. As he began to get older, he tried to get rid of the fear that would come upon him by drinking heavily. This of course made things much worse. He said that just two years ago he had ended up drunk while he was driving his motorcycle. This resulted in him having a terrible and life-threatening accident. In this motorcycle accident, his head injury was so bad that it had left him blind in his left eye and deaf in his left ear.

The medical world informed him there was no help for his eye or his ear because of his head injury that he experienced in a motorcycle accident. In his left eye, there was no pupil and nothing to be seen but white. He also informed me that for the last two years his left ear had no discernible sound but a constant irritating hissing.

I shared my testimony with Todd about how God had delivered me, save my soul, and completely healed my body. I gave him my book "Living in the Realm of the Miraculous", encouraging him to read it, to build up his faith. I asked him if he had ever given his heart to Jesus Christ. He responded that he had never done such a thing, or ever been invited to do this. I then informed him that I would like to pray over him, and ask God to give him a miracle. He agreed to allow me to pray for him.

I laid my left hand over his blind eye and my right hand over his deaf ear. **I spoke the name of Jesus Christ, and commanded the blind spirit, and deaf spirit to come out right now by the authority of Christ.** Then I spoke a creative miracle to his blind eye and his death ear, commanding them to be restored in the name of Jesus Christ of Nazareth. I did not speak, or pray very loud in the name of Jesus, but I simply spoke with authority, and with the compassion of Christ for this man.

When I removed my hands from his head, he looked like he was in complete shock. He informed me that the moment I spoke in the name of Jesus that there was a loud popping sound in his left ear. He exclaimed with excitement that this was the first time he had heard any other type of noise other than the hissing sound that he had heard for the last two years. I told him to examine his hearing a little more, and then he told me with complete shock that all of the existing hissing sounds was completely gone.

I had him cover his good ear with his left hand. Then I bent down to his ear and whispered the name of Jesus approximately four times. He did not know exactly what I was saying, but would say Yesis, repeatedly. Then I began to say other things in his ear, which caused him to begin to cry and shake. He could not believe it, but God had opened up his ear, and repairable his damaged left deaf ear.

I shared the gospel with him in a much deeper way now that I had is complete and total undivided attention. When I was done speaking the reality of Christ to him, I asked him if he would like to give his heart to Jesus Christ? He told me that he was ready to not only accept Christ but to surrender his life to him. He was shaking under the power of God as I lead him into a prayer of salvation.

He informed me that he would begin to attend our church services, and kept thank me, and hugged me twice. I informed him that it was Jesus Christ who had healed him, and made him whole, and that I was nobody special. I left him standing in his room shaking and crying saying: thank you, Jesus, thank you, God.

*29. He Was a Pedophile (2008)

I have a house where I rent at a very low price to single men. These men are either on assistance, getting out of jail, or even homeless. My whole purpose is to help them get back on their feet or to help them assimilate back into society. Now to rent from me, there are certain criteria that you have to meet. My house is in a residential area so I never rent to anybody who I would consider a danger to the community. There was an older gentleman who came to me who wanted to rent a room. Something in my heart told me he was a pedophile. I asked him straight out if he was on Megan's list or if he had ever committed a sexual crime! He assured me that he was not on Megan's list; neither had he ever committed a sexual crime.

Now we also had a house that was close to our church that we would rent to those who seem to be hungry for God. This older gentleman wanted to attend our church and move down to this house to be close to the church. I set up an appointment for him to come and look at one of the rooms that we have available. When he arrived at our property my son Daniel was standing there with me. The minute he saw this gentleman, Dan became extremely upset. I told this man to go ahead into the house, and I would be with him in a minute.

I asked my son what was wrong. He said, "Dad: I just had a vision of this man!" I said: "Okay, tell me what you saw." He said, "Dad: this man is a pedophile!" I said, "Dan you've got to be wrong." I told him that I also had thought there was something wrong with him in this area, but I asked him point-blank if he was on Megan's list, or if he had ever messed around with children. He declared that he had not. Dan told me that he had an open vision, and in this open vision, he saw this man chasing a little girl who was around six years old.

My son Daniel continued to insist that what he saw was of God, and I needed to check it out. I told him: okay, let me talk to him. I went into the house where this man was looking at one of the rooms. I came right out and said to him, "Harvey I asked you before if you had ever committed a sexual crime, or if you were on Megan's list. I am asking you again: have you ever committed a sexual crime?" He hung his head down and whispered: I lied, I do have a record of committing a sexual crime.

Because of my son's open vision, I asked him: who was it? With his head hung down, he said: my six-year-old niece. Now you might say, Pastor isn't there forgiveness for sexual crimes? Yes, there is! But from my experience of almost forty years of pastoring, there is such a strong demonic spirit involved in this act, that unless a person truly repents with all their heart, and cries out to God for complete deliverance, they never get free. Yes, we forgive, but we must also protect our loved ones. May God give us spiritual discernment!

CHAPTER ELEVEN

Truths That Will Set You Free!

In this chapter, I would simply like to clarify some significant truths that will help you not to become ensnared with foolishness. I have run into many people in the last 40 years that thought they had some deep spiritual insight in dealing with the demonic world. Most of this stuff is nothing but rabbit trails, dead and alleys, just foolish and ridiculous crusades.

People get to focusing on subject matters that are not going to make a difference. Instead of focusing on Jesus Christ and preaching the reality of who he is, what he has done, and what has been made available to us, they focus on the enemy. I think a good example of this was when Paul the apostle was on Mars Hill. Please notice that he did not spend any time exposing, or going into great detail about the doctrines or the belief systems that they were foolishly trusting in. What did he do? He preached Jesus Christ! The enemy loves to get us off the reality of who Christ is! If you look up the word preach In the Book of Acts, you will discover they constantly were preaching Jesus Christ. They were preaching Jesus Christ and that there is repentance, remission, salvation, healing, salvation, deliverance, atonement and freedom found only in Jesus! We will look at 15 versus in order see how we should be dealing with people who have been deceived by false religions, and line spirits.

Acts 17:16 Now while Paul waited for them at Athens, his spirit was stirred in him, when he saw the city wholly given to idolatry.17 Therefore disputed he in the synagogue with the Jews, and with the devout persons, and in the market daily with

them that met with him.18 Then certain philosophers of the Epicureans, and of the Stoicks, encountered him. And some said, What will this babbler say? other some, He seemeth to be a setter forth of strange gods: because he preached unto them Jesus, and the resurrection.19 And they took him, and brought him unto Areopagus, saying, May we know what this new doctrine, whereof thou speakest, is?20 For thou bringest certain strange things to our ears: we would know therefore what these things mean.21 (For all the Athenians and strangers which were there spent their time in nothing else, but either to tell, or to hear some new thing.)22 Then Paul stood in the midst of Mars' hill, and said, Ye men of Athens, I perceive that in all things ye are too superstitious.23 For as I passed by, and beheld your devotions, I found an altar with this inscription, To The Unknown God. Whom therefore ye ignorantly worship, him declare I unto you.24 God that made the world and all things therein, seeing that he is Lord of heaven and earth, dwelleth not in temples made with hands;25 Neither is worshipped with men's hands, as though he needed anything, seeing he giveth to all life, and breath, and all things;26 And hath made of one blood all nations of men for to dwell on all the face of the earth, and hath determined the times before appointed, and the bounds of their habitation;*27 That they should seek the Lord, if haply they might feel after him, and find him, though he be not far from every one of us:28 For in him we live, and move, and have our being; as certain also of your own poets have said, For we are also his offspring.29 Forasmuch then as we are the offspring of God, we ought not to think that the Godhead is like unto gold, or silver, or stone, graven by art and man's device.30 And the times of this ignorance* God winked at; but now commandeth all men everywhere to repent:*31 Because he hath appointed a day, in the which he will judge the world in righteousness by that man whom he hath ordained; whereof he hath given assurance unto all men, in that he hath raised him from the dead.*

Please notice that Paul did not go into a never ending speech are teaching about their religions are the belief systems.

Now, why would I say this? That you do not waste your time attacking or exposing **Mormonism, Hinduism, Freemasons, witchcraft, cultic activities** or any of these other items. You might say: **What?** Yes, you heard me right. But don't they have to renounce and come out of these things? Yes, just as much as they have to any of the other works of the flesh found in Galatians 5, and other locations in the New Testament. These are all manifestations of the flesh. If someone tells me that there is a witch in my meeting, it does not change my preaching in the least. One of two things will happen. #1 as I am preaching they will get up and leave. #2 the demons will manifest themselves, and I will cast them out.

If a person is truly touched and converted by the power of God, they will repent of all known sin. Once they are truly converted, they will hunger and thirst after God, and read their Bibles and will continue to repent, coming out of every sin that the Spirit of God and the word of God reveals to them. I only make this statement because I have met many people who major on the minors, and minor on the majors. What is the major? It is Jesus Christ and him alone! It is a complete and absolute abandonment to his will, his plan, his nature, and his purposes for our life. You cannot show me in the New Testament were people who were delivered were taken through some long process to renounce, to recant everything they were involved in. Before I got born again, I was involved in a lot of wicked and stupid stuff, but when I fell to my knees and repented that Jesus, I was forgiven and made brand-new. When I stood up upon my feet on that day of February 18, at 3 PM, 1975, I was a brand-new creature, a new creation.

What about the Removing of Statues, Pictures, Taxidermy, Crucifix, etc.

If you go on the Internet, you will discover websites

everywhere dedicated to believers removing a never ending list all kinds of items from their houses and our lives. I call them witch hunts, dead-end trails, never ending rabbit trails, and endeavors of spirituality. Their whole mindset becomes obsessed with ridding their lives of those things which are expressions of the world, the flesh, and the devil. **Yes**, there are items we definitely should get rid of. The Holy Spirit will lead us into all truth. Anything that is obviously wicked, sexually alluring, violent in nature, should be dealt with. All of the other artifacts do not mean a thing. And to the real believer, they do not mean a thing. In the Old Testament in the book of Leviticus the descendants of Abraham were not allowed to have anything around them that expressed nature. The reason for this was that they were not born again. They easily went astray after the flesh. In the New Testament, we are born again, filled with the Holy Spirit, with the law of God written in our heart and our minds. We have overcome the world because greater is he that is in us than he that is in the world.

To be honest, anything can lead us astray if our hearts are not right with God. It could be your car, your house, sports, hobbies, your job, and even the person you love. So, are you going to get rid of these items in your life? The minute we take our eyes off of Jesus Christ, we will go astray. Jesus said: if a man does not abide in me, he is like a branch that is no longer attached to the vine. This person will dry up, and the only thing he'll be good for is to be thrown into the fire. It is in our DNA to worship, and if we are not worshiping Christ alone, we cannot help but worship something. Carnally minded people love to make mountains out of mole hills. And yet these are the very people that are writing and selling books, trying to make things mystical, powerful, and other worldly, things that have no significance. Here's an example:

*30. Carnality Disguised As Spirituality!

As a pastor since 1977, I have had many people come through the churches I have pastored and started. Back in about 2005, I had one family with the relatives who began to attend our church. It turns out that they were followers of those who propagated these doctrines of looking high and low for the devil everywhere. It seemed like there was a devil behind every doorknob. Their minds are so caught up in trying to find the devil; they could not see Jesus. At times I have had people stand up and begin to brag about the devil during a church service. I lovingly tell him that the devil has no place here, and they need to exalt Christ or sit down. We are not going to exalt the devil in our church services. We are here to exalt Jesus Christ.

Back to the story: this family and its members began to influence the congregation to rid their house of anything that they thought was evil. One of the sisters of the church who had been attending our fellowship since she was a young girl back in the early 80s informed me that they had been to her house. They had gone to her house and had stripped it of every statue they could find. They had stripped her house of pictures which had nothing to do with the devil or demonic activity. If there was a statue of a frog, or and owl they threw it into a healing pile outside of the front porch of her house. There was no spirituality or power in these people's lives. In their minds, they thought they were spiritual giants. I'm not attacking these people; I am just pointing out the fact that there are many things being propagated as being spirituality when all reality it is carnality.

I did not attack this family, or say anything over the pulpit about what they had done with the sister of our church at her house. I minister to them to the extent I could in their carnality. It was not very long before they were causing a lot of strife in the church. It turns out there was a strong spirit of religiosity, bitterness, and pride running deep in their lives. You will discover that this is usually the case with people who run after these doctrines. All you can do is be loving, gentle and patient with them, Per adventure they will recover themselves out of the snare of the devil who have taken them captive because of their silly ideals. They eventually left the church leaving destruction in their wake. I have seen people like this produce the same fruit wherever they go. They are totally convinced that they are spiritual and that anybody who does not agree with them is under the control of the devil. These type of people are always very controlling and manipulative, and yet they do not know what spirit they are of.

What should I do if I find myself in the midst of this kind of people? Run from them as fast as you can. They are not going to take you into a deep walk with Jesus Christ. They will never operate in the power and the authority of Jesus. Instead of setting people free, they will bring people into bondage into their carnality.

Do I Have To Know the Devil's Names?

There are so many wrong teachings when it comes to exorcism. The things that I'm sharing with you in this book are from my personal experiences and biblical studies. My theology, philosophy, and doctrines have been formulated by the New Testament and the life of Christ. I'm not saying that everything I am teaching is absolute truth because we all can be deceived without knowing it. The first four years of my life as a Christian I spent all my time in the four Gospels. As I studied the **life of Jesus,** it created within me an amazing understanding of the will of the father. Hebrews chapter 1 boldly declares that Jesus Christ is the express image and will of the Heavenly Father! There is an amazing amount of Scriptures of Jesus Christ casting out evil spirits. Jesus is my supreme example of how to deal with the devil.

Did Jesus Ask Their Names?

Yes, **One Time**. Did you hear that? Jesus asked **one time** who the demon was. It is revealed to us from approximately 100 instances where we see Jesus and the disciples dealing with evil entities that only **one time** were they ever asked their names. And when you look at that situation you'll discover that they said that they were legion which simply means many.

Luke 8:29 (For he JESUS, had commanded the unclean spirit to come out of the man. For oftentimes it had caught him: and he was kept bound with chains and in fetters; and he brake the bands, and was driven of the devil into the wilderness.)30 And Jesus asked him, saying, What is thy name? And he said, Legion: because many devils were entered into him.31 And they besought him that he would not command them to go out into the deep.

Amazingly you never see Jesus giving specific names to the Devils he was casting out. As you study the Scriptures, you'll discover he used general terms for these invisible evil entities. People love to get fancy, sophisticated, supposedly spiritual with the names that they tag upon certain devils. I simply would not waste my time with this line of thinking. It is not my right to add or take away from the Scriptures. I simply deal with them the way that Jesus did. I have never had a problem in casting out a devil simply by calling it what it is. For instance, if the person is deaf and cannot speak, I tell the deaf and dumb spirit to come out. The power is not in the name of this evil entity, but the power is in the name of **Jesus Christ**! Many times Jesus simply called them Unclean Spirits

Matthew 10:1 And when he had called unto him his twelve disciples, he gave them power against **unclean spirits,** *to cast them out, and to heal all manner of sickness and all manner of disease.*

Matthew 12:43 When the **unclean spirit** *is gone out of a man, he walketh through dry places, seeking rest, and findeth none.*

Mark 1:23 And there was in their synagogue a man with an

unclean spirit; *and he cried out,*

Mark 1:26 And when the unclean spirit *had torn him, and cried with a loud voice, he came out of him.*

Mark 1:27 And they were all amazed, insomuch that they questioned among themselves, saying, What thing is this? what new doctrine is this? for with authority commandeth he even the unclean spirits, *and they do obey him.*

Mark 3:11 And unclean spirits, *when they saw him, fell down before him, and cried, saying, Thou art the Son of God.*

Mark 3:30 Because they said, He hath an unclean spirit.

Mark 5:2 And when he was come out of the ship, immediately there met him out of the tombs a man with an unclean spirit,

---

Mark 5:8 For he said unto him, Come out of the man, thou unclean spirit.

Mark 5:13 And forthwith Jesus gave them leave. And the unclean spirits *went out, and entered into the swine: and the herd ran violently down a steep place into the sea, (they were about two thousand;) and were choked in the sea.*

Mark 6:7 And he called unto him the twelve, and began to send them forth by two and two; and gave them power over unclean spirits;

Mark 7:25 For a certain woman, whose young daughter had an unclean spirit, *heard of him, and came and fell at his feet:*

Luke 4:33 And in the synagogue there was a man, which had a spirit of an **unclean devil,** *and cried out with a loud voice,*

Acts 5:16 There came also a multitude out of the cities round about unto Jerusalem, bringing sick folks, and them which were vexed with **unclean spirits***: and they were healed every one.*

Acts 8:7 For **unclean spirits,** *crying with loud voice, came out of many that were possessed with them: and many taken with palsies, and that were lame, were healed.*

Here are other examples of simply calling the spirits by what they do!

1 Kings 22:22 And the Lord said unto him, Wherewith? And he said, I will go forth, and I will be a **lying spirit** *in the mouth of all his prophets. And he said, Thou shalt persuade him, and prevail also: go forth, and do so.*

Luke 7:21 And in that same hour he cured many of their infirmities and plagues, and of **evil spirits;** *and unto many that were blind he gave sight.*

Mark 9:25 When Jesus saw that the people came running together, he rebuked the **foul spirit,** *saying unto him, Thou* **dumb and deaf spirit,** *I charge thee, come out of him, and enter no more into him.*

Devils Are Liars and Deceivers! You Cannot Believe a Word They Say!

John 8:44 Ye are of your father the devil, and the lusts of your father ye will do. He was a murderer from the beginning, and abode not in the truth, because there is no truth in him. When he speaketh a lie, he speaketh of his own: for he is a liar, and the father of it.

Revelation 12:9 And the great dragon was cast out, that old serpent, called the Devil, and Satan, which deceiveth the whole world: he was cast out into the earth, and his angels were cast out with him.

---

2 Corinthians 11:3 But I fear, lest by any means, as the serpent beguiled Eve through his subtilty, so your minds should be corrupted from the simplicity that is in Christ.

---

2 Thessalonians 2:9 Even him, whose coming is after the working of Satan with all power and signs and lying wonders,10 And with all deceivableness of unrighteousness in them that perish; because they received not the love of the truth, that they might be saved.11 And for this cause God shall send them strong delusion, that they should believe a lie:

So what can we conclude out of this study? That we do not need to waste our time trying to find out the names of these Devils and evil entities. In an upcoming chapter, I will be sharing approximately 24 experiences that Smith Wigglesworth (an amazing man of God) had with casting out Devils. You would discover that many times he never even mentioned what kind of spirit it was. He simply said: **Come Out In Jesus Name!**

Acts 16:18 And this did she many days. But Paul, being grieved, turned and said to the spirit, I command thee in the name of Jesus Christ to come out of her. And he came out the same hour.

Do Not Carry on a Conversation With Evil Spirits!

You should never carry on a conversation with the demonic powers you are casting out of people. **First** remember that they are liars, and there is no truth in them. You cannot believe a word they say. **Second,** they love to be entertained. They are starving for attention and worship. Lucifer wanted to be God, to be worshiped, to be exalted, to be idolized. All of the angelic and spiritual entities that followed him became corrupted with the same spiritual disease called sin.

Matthew 4:9 And saith unto him, All these things will I give thee, if thou wilt fall and worship me.:10 Then saith Jesus unto him, Get thee hence, Satan: for it is written, Thou shalt worship the Lord thy God, and him only shalt thou serve.

I never let the Devils exalt themselves when I'm dealing with them. If you are where you need to be spiritually, you simply should be able to tell them to **shut up**, and to **come out, Now in Jesus Name!**

*Mark 1:34 And he healed many that were sick of divers diseases, and cast out many devils; and **suffered not the devils to speak because they knew him.***

Those in the deliverance ministry who are letting the devil speak are actually putting themselves into a very dangerous position. **The Scripture absolutely forbids us to give place to the devil.** Unbeknownst to them, they are giving into a lying and deceiving spirit. The **Third** reality is that the Devils in those we are casting them out of want to deceive the one that God is using to cast them out. I do not need to ask them questions, because they have nothing that I really need to know from them. It is the Holy Ghost that brings me into all truth. The Holy Ghost tells me in every situation what is going on. **The Holy Ghost Is the Spirit of Truth.** The spirit or spirits I am dealing with are nothing but liars, thieves, murderers of the innocent. I do not have any time to mess around with them, or listen to what they have to say. If you have been entertaining evil spirits as you cast them out: **STOP IT and**

REPENT! Do not ever allow evil spirits to exalt themselves. Here is a True Story from **Kenneth E Hagin** who I use to work for.

Jesus Appeared To Kenneth E. Hagin

In December 1952, in Broken Bow, OK Jesus appeared to Hagin. Jesus said to him, **"I have come to teach you concerning the devil, demons and demon possession. I will show you how these spirits get hold of people and dominate them – even Christians, if they allow them to."**

At this time in Kenneth Hagins life, he did not have the revelation that he had authority over Satan and demons. Up until this point, he had prayed to Jesus or God the Father to do something about the devil for him.

How Evil Spirits Get Hold Of People

In the vision of Jesus, Kenneth E. Hagin suddenly saw a woman. He recognized her as being the former wife of a pastor. He had been introduced to her and her husband on one occasion. Other than that, he had no communication with them but had since learned that she had left her husband.

The Lord Jesus said to a Hagin, "This woman was a child of mine, she was in the ministry with her husband. She was filled with the Spirit, and the gifts of the Spirit were operating in her life. One day an evil spirit came to her and whispered in her ear, you are a beautiful woman. You could have had fame, popularity, and wealth, but you have been cheated in life by following the Christian walk. The woman realized that this was an evil spirit, and she said, "Get thee behind me, Satan." The spirit left her for a period.

By and by the same spirit returned. He sat on her shoulder and whispered in her ear; you are a beautiful woman, but you have been robbed by taking this lowly walk of Christianity and living a separated life. Again she recognized this as Satan. She said, "Satan, I resist you in the Name of Jesus" and he left her for a while.

But he came back again and sat on her shoulder, whispering the same things in her ear. This time, she began to entertain these thoughts, for she liked to think that she was beautiful. As she began to think along the lines the devil suggested to her, she became obsessed with that thinking."

Satan's Oppression, Obsession, Possession

In the vision, Kenneth Hagin saw the woman turn as transparent as glass, and he saw a black dot in her mind. Jesus told him that the black dot represented how she was obsessed in her thinking with that spirit. Jesus told him at First she was oppressed on the outside, but she allowed the devil's suggestions to take hold of her.

Her mind became obsessed with that spirit. She wanted to think that she was beautiful and could have had fame, wealth, and popularity and that she had been robbed of life by becoming a Christian.

Jesus told Hagin that she could have resisted and refused to think those thoughts and the evil spirit would have fled. But she chose to yield to the **evil spirit**. Finally, the woman left her husband and went out into the world seeking the fame and wealth the devil offered her. She took up with one man after another. She told the Lord Jesus Christ to leave her alone and that she did not want Him anymore. After a time, that **evil spirit** moved from her head to her soul, and she became possessed by that **evil spirit**. Kenneth E. Hagin saw the black dot move from her head to her spirit.

Command The Harassment To Stop

In the vision, Hagin asked the Lord, "Why have you shown me this vision. Do you want me to cast the evil spirit out of her?" Jesus said, **"No, you couldn't cast it out of her because she wants that spirit and as long as she wants it, she can have it, and you can't make it leave."** Jesus told him he wanted him to take authority over this evil spirit because it was operating through her, harassing and intimidating the ministry of her former husband. Jesus taught him there was no distance in the realm of the spirit and Hagin commanded the spirit to stop harassing this minister through this woman, in the **Name of Jesus**. It stopped, and the minister was never harassed by this evil spirit again.

Spend Eternity In The Regions Of The Damned

Kenneth E. Hagin asked the Lord what would happen to this woman. Jesus said, **"She will spend eternity in the regions of the damned, where there is weeping and gnashing of teeth."** In the vision, he saw her go down into the pit of hell and heard her awful screams. Papa Hagin said to the Lord, "This woman was your child and filled with the Spirit and had a part in the ministry. You said for me not to pray for her. I cannot understand this!"

The Sin Unto Death

The Lord reminded Hagin of the following Scripture: "If any man sees his brother sin a sin which is not unto death, he shall ask, and he shall give him life for them that sin, not unto death. There is a sin unto death: I do not say that he shall pray for it." (1 John 5:16) He said to the Lord, "I have always believed that the sin referred to in this Scripture is physical death and that the person is saved although he has sinned." The Lord pointed out to him that the Scripture didn't say physical death, and that Hagin was adding something to it.

Jesus continued, "If you read the entire fifth chapter of First

John, you will see that it is talking about life and death – spiritual life and spiritual death. This refers to a believer who can sin a sin unto death, and therefore I say that you shall not pray for it. I told you not to pray for this woman because she sinned a sin unto death." Hagin told the Lord that this disrupted his theology and would He explain it some more?

Jesus Teaches About The Sin Unto Death

Jesus reminded Kenneth Hagin about the scriptures found in Hebrews 6:4-6. Hagin told the Lord that his denomination taught that those "once enlightened" in that verse did not refer to Christians, but it was talking about lost people who get under conviction.

The Lord said, "Remember I told you this woman was my child. She was filled with the Holy Spirit, and she had a part in the ministry. You will notice that the scripture says, 'It is impossible for those who were once enlightened, and have tasted of the heavenly gift…' I am the heavenly gift. A man under conviction is enlightened, but he has not tasted of me. Jesus reminded him of John 3:16 and Romans 6:23. Jesus said, **"No one has tasted the heavenly gift until he has accepted Me as Lord and Savior."** Hebrews 6:4-5, said, 'made partakers of the Holy Ghost.' Jesus told him that this lady had been baptized in the Holy Ghost and had tasted the good Word of God. Jesus told him that baby Christians could not commit the sin unto death.

Steps To The Sin Unto Death

The **first step** to the sin unto death is for one to see their lost state and know that Jesus is the only way of salvation. The **second step** is to receive Jesus or be born again. The **third step** is to be filled with the Holy Ghost. The **fourth step** is to have grown out of the babyhood stage of Christianity and tasted the good Word of God. The **fifth step** is to have the gifts of the Spirit operating in their life. Jesus pointed out to Dad Hagin the following scriptures,

Hebrews 6:6; 10:26-29.

Jesus explained the last step in the following words. Jesus said, "It is sad that this woman left her husband for another man, but adultery is not the unpardonable sin. If she had turned back to Me in repentance, even though she might have had a hundred men, I would have forgiven her. Whatever she might have done, if she had asked Me to forgive her, I would have.
"Even if she had been a baby Christian when she said, I don't want Jesus anymore; leave me alone,' and didn't realize what she was doing, I would have forgiven her. If she had done that because she was tempted and pressed beyond measure, I would forgive her.

But she knew exactly what she was doing, and she acted willfully when she said, 'I don't want the Lord Jesus anymore.' I merely showed you this so you might see how the devil can get hold of Christians if they permit him too."

We Must Command Evil Spirits To Go

In the vision, a little demon ran between Kenneth Hagin and Jesus. The demon put out a smoke screen, and Dad Hagin could not see Jesus. Then the demon started yelling so that Hagin could not hear Jesus. He thought, Doesn't the Lord know I am missing what He is saying? I need to get that – it is important – but I am missing it. He waited for Jesus to do something about the demon, but He didn't do anything. Finally, in desperation Hagin commanded the demon to be quiet, in the **Name of Jesus Christ!** The demon stopped and fell to the floor, and the smoke screen disappeared. The demon lay there whimpering, and Hagin commanded the demon to leave, and it got up and ran away.

Kenneth Hagin's Theology Was Changed By Jesus

In the vision, Dad Hagin was still wondering why Jesus had not stopped the evil spirit from interfering. Jesus knew what Kenneth Hagin was thinking. He said If you hadn't done something about that I couldn't have." Dad Hagin responded and said, "Lord I know I misunderstood you! You said you couldn't do anything about it, but you really meant to say that you wouldn't." Jesus said, **"No if you hadn't done something about that spirit I couldn't have."** Hagin said, "But Lord, You can do anything. To say you couldn't is different than anything I have ever preached or heard preached. That really upends my theology." The Lord said, "Sometimes your theology needs upending."

The Believer Must Rebuke The Devil

Jesus taught him that nowhere in the New Testament is the believer told to pray for God to do something about the devil for them. The believer is always told to take **authority over the devil**. Jesus proved it to Hagin with these scriptures: *Matthew 28:18-20, Mark 16:17, James 4:7, 1 Peter 5:8-9, Ephesian 4:27.*
You need to take authority over the devil of your life, church, ministry, community and the government. Victory is surely yours as you use the authority that Jesus gave to you over Satan, in the Name of Jesus!

Dr Michael H Yeager

CHAPTER TWELVE

CASTING OUT DEVILS - I
By Smith Wigglesworth!

All of these true testimonies of Smith Wigglesworth comes from the book that I wrote called: The Miracles of Smith Wigglesworth. This book can be purchased on Amazon.

Smith Wigglesworth was Born June 10th, 1859 and Died March 4th, 1947. He began as a Methodist; he became a born again Christian at the age of eight. His Bible teaching came from the Plymouth Brethren while learning the plumbing trade as an apprentice from a man in the Brethren movement.[1]

Wigglesworth married Polly Featherstone on 2 May 1882. She was a preacher with the Salvation Army. Wigglesworth learned to read after he married Polly; she taught him to read the Bible. He often stated that it was the only book he ever read, and did not permit newspapers in his home, preferring the Bible to be their only reading material.

Wigglesworth worked as a plumber, but he abandoned this trade because he was too busy for it after he started preaching. He became used of God after he was baptized in the Holy Ghost, and speaking in tongues.

Smith - "The Bible is the Word of God: supernatural in origin, eternal in duration, inexpressible in valor, infinite in scope, regenerative in power, infallible in authority, universal in interest, personal in application, inspired in totality. Read it through, write it down, pray it in, work it out, and then pass it on. Truly it is the Word of God. It brings into man the personality of God; it changes the man until he becomes the epistle of God. It transforms his mind, changes his character, takes him on from grace to grace, and gives him an inheritance in the Spirit. God comes in, dwells in walks in, talks through, and sups with him."

Sermon: Spiritual Power

#16   A woman came to me in Cardiff, Wales, who was filled with an ulceration. She had fallen in the streets twice through this trouble. She came to the meeting, and it seemed as if the evil power within her was trying to kill her right there, for she fell, and the power of the devil was extremely brutal. She was helpless, and it seemed as if she had died right there on the spot. I cried,

"O God, help this woman." **Then I rebuked the evil power in the name of Jesus,** and instantly right then and there the Lord healed her. She rose up and was so filled with excitement and joy that we could not keep her quiet. She felt the power of God in her body and wanted to testify all the time. After three days she went to another place and began to testify about the Lord's power to heal the sick and the demonically oppressed. She came to me and said, "I want to tell everyone about the Lord's healing power. Have you no tracts on this subject?" I handed her my Bible and said, "Matthew, Mark, Luke, John--they are the best tracts on healing. They are full of incidents about the power of Jesus. They will never fail to accomplish the work of God if people will believe them."

Smith - "You must be yielded to the Word of God. The Word will

cause love to begin to flow in our hearts like a River, and when divine love is in our hearts, there is no room to boast about ourselves. We see ourselves as nothing when we get lost in this divine love."

#19   A man came to me one time, brought to me by a little woman. I said, "What's going on with him?" She said, "He gets into circumstances of being attempted, but he fails every time. He is a slave to alcohol and nicotine poison. He is a bright, intelligent man in most things, but he just gives in to those two things." I was reminded of the words of the Master, giving us the power to bind and loose, and I told him to put out his tongue.

In **the name of the Lord Jesus Christ, I cast out the evil powers** that gave him the taste for these things. I said to him, "Sir, you are free from today forward." He was unsaved, but when he realized the power of the Lord had delivered him, he came to our meetings. He publicly acknowledged that he was a sinner, and the Lord saved and baptized him right then and there. A few days later I asked, "How are things going with you?" He said, "I am delivered." **God has given us the power to bind and the power to loose even the spirit of alcohol and nicotine**. But in order to operate in this authority, you must be submitted to that authority, the Lordship of Jesus Christ.

Smith - As we think about that which is Holy, we become Holy. The more we think about Jesus, the more we become like Him.

#29   In Switzerland the people said to me, "How long can you preach to us?" I said to them, "When the Holy Ghost is upon us, we can preach forever!" When I was in San Francisco, driving down the main street one day, we came across a crowd in the street. The driver stopped, and I jumped out of the car, and right across from where the tumult was, I found a boy lying on the ground apparently in the grip of death. I got down and asked,

"What is amiss?" He replied in a whisper, "tramp." I put my hand underneath his back and said, **"In the name of Jesus, come out."** And the boy jumped up and ran away, not even stopping to say "Thank you."

Smith - "I know that God's word is sufficient. One word from Him can change a nation. His word is from everlasting to everlasting. It is through the entrance of this everlasting Word, this incorruptible seed, that we are born again, and come into this wonderful salvation. Man cannot live by bread alone, but must live by every word that proceeded out of the mouth of God. This is the food of faith. "Faith cometh by hearing, and hearing by the Word of God."

#32 In a place in England I was teaching on the lines of faith and what would take place if we believed God. Many wonderful things were happening. When I was done teaching, it appeared one man who worked in a coal mine had heard me. He was in trouble with a very stiff knee. He said to his wife, "I cannot help but think every day that that message of Wigglesworth's was to stir us to do something. I cannot get it out of my mind. All the men in the pit know how I walk with a stiff knee, and you know how you have wrapped it around with yards of flannel.

Well, I am going to act. You have to be the congregation." He got his wife in front of him. "I am going to act and do just as Wigglesworth did." He got hold of his leg unmercifully, saying, **"Come out, you devils, come out! In the name of Jesus.** Now, Jesus, help me. **Come out, you devils, come out."** Then he said, "Wife they are gone! Wife, they are gone. This is too good. I am going to act now." So he went to his place of worship, and all the other coal workers were there. It was a prayer meeting. As he told them this story these men became delighted. They said, "Jack, come over here and help me." And Jack went. As soon as he was through in one home, he was invited to another, delivering and losing these people of the pains they had gotten in the coal mine.

Smith - Be filled to overflowing with the Spirit. We are no good if we have only a full cup; we need to have an OVERFLOWING cup!

Sermon: After you have received power

#35   One day as I came into the house my wife said, "Which way did you come?" I answered that I had come in by the back way. "Oh," she said, "if you had come in by the front you would have seen a man there in a terrible state. There is a crowd of people around him, and he is in terrible condition." Then the doorbell rang, and she said, "There he is again. What shall we do?" I said, "Just be still." I rushed to the door and just as I was opening it the Spirit said, "This is what I baptized you for." I was very careful then in opening the door, and then I heard the man crying outside, "Oh I have committed the unpardonable sin, I am lost, I am lost."

I asked him to come in, and when he got inside, he said again in awful distress, "I am lost, I am lost." Then the Spirit came upon me, and **I commanded the lying spirit to come out of the man in the name of Jesus.** Suddenly he lifted up his arms and said, "I never did it." The moment the **lying spirit was out of him,** he was able to speak the truth. I then realized the power in the Baptism of the Holy Spirit. It was the Spirit that said, "This is what I baptized you for," and I believe we ought to be in the place where we shall always be able to understand the mind of the Spirit amid all the other voices in the world.

Smith - Before a man can bind the enemy, he must know there is nothing binding him.

#36 One day as I was waiting for a taxi I stepped into a shoemaker's shop. I had not been there long when I saw a man with a green shade over his eyes, crying pitifully and in great agony. It was heart-rending, and the Shoemaker told me that the inflammation was burning out his eyes. I jumped up and went to the man and said, **"You devil, come out of this man in the name of Jesus."** Instantly the man said, "It is all gone, the pain has left, and I can see now." That is the only Scriptural way, to touch the lives of people, and then preach afterwards. You will find as the days go by that the miracles and healings will be manifested. Because the Master was touched with the feeling of the infirmities of the multitudes they instantly gathered around Him to hear what He had to say concerning the Word of God. However, I would rather see one man saved than ten thousand people healed.

Smith - God wants to give you a faith that shakes hell!

#49 A woman came to be healed of a terrible cancer. How it did smell—but God healed her instantly. The husband got saved and the whole family with him. I believe there is a crown for all believers, but it will have to be fought for. There was a young woman vomiting blood. God awakened me in the middle of the night, and in the **Name of Jesus I commanded the demon power to come out**, and she was immediately healed. It is all in the precious name of Jesus Christ.

Smith - There are boundless possibilities for you if you dare to believe.

Sermon: By faith

#53   I remember one night, being in the north of England and going around to see some sick people, I was taken into a house where there was a young woman lying on her bed, a very helpless case. Her reason was gone, and many things were manifested that were absolutely Satanic, and I knew it.

She was a beautiful young woman. Her husband was quite a young man. He came in with a baby in his arms, leaned over and kissed his wife. The moment he did so, she threw herself over on the other side of the bed, just as a lunatic would do, with no consciousness of the presence of her husband. It was heart-breaking, The husband took the baby and pressed the baby's lips to the mother. Again there was a wild frenzy. I said, to the sister who was attending her, "Have you anybody to help?" She answered, "We have done everything we could." I said, "Have you no spiritual help?" Her husband stormed and said, "Spiritual help? Do you think we believe in God after we have had seven weeks of no sleep and this maniac condition? If you think we believe in God, you are mistaken. You have come to the wrong house."

There was a young woman about eighteen who grinned at me as she passed out of the door, as much as to say, "You cannot do anything." But this brought me to a place of compassion for this poor young woman. And then with what faith I had, I began to penetrate the heavens. I was soon out on the heights, and I tell you I never saw a man get anything from God who prayed on the earth level. If you get anything from God, you will have to pray right into heaven, for all you want is there. If you are living an earthly life, all taken up with sensual things, and expect things from heaven, they will never come. God wants us to be a heavenly people, seated with Him in the heavenlies, and laying hold of all the things in heaven that are at our disposal.

I saw there, in the presence of that demented girl, limitations to my faith; but as I prayed there came to another faith into my heart that could not be denied, a faith that grasped the promises, a faith that believed God's Word. I came from the presence of the glory back to earth. I was not the same man. I confronted the same conditions I had seen before, but in the name of Jesus. With a faith that could shake hell and move anything else, I cried to the demon power that was making this young woman a maniac, **"Come out of her, in the name of Jesus!"** She rolled over and fell asleep, and awakened in fourteen hours, perfectly sane and perfectly whole.

Smith - "Repeat in your heart often: "baptized with the Holy Ghost and fire, fire, fire!" All the unction, and weeping, and travailing comes through the baptism of fire, and I say to you and say to myself, purged and cleansed and filled with renewed spiritual power." *"Who makes his ministers a flame of fire." Heb. 1:7*

#62   I was traveling one day in a railway train in Sweden. At one station there boarded the train an old lady with her daughter. The old lady's expression was so troubled that I enquired what the matter with her was. I heard that she was going to the hospital to have her leg taken off. She began to weep as she told that the doctors had said there was no hope for her except through having her leg amputated. She was seventy years old. I said to my interpreter, "Tell her that Jesus can heal her." The instant this was said to her, it was as though a veil was taken off her face, it became so light. We stopped at another station, and the carriage filled up with people. There was a rush of men to board that train and the devil said, "You're done for now. There's no way you can pray with all of these people here" But I knew I had God working with me, for hard things are always opportunities to give the Lord more glory when He manifests His power. Every trial is a blessing.

There have been times when I have been pressed through circumstances, and it seemed as if a dozen road engines were going over me, but I have found that the hardest things are just the right opportunities for the grace of God to work. We have such a lovely Jesus. He always proves Himself to be such a mighty Deliverer. He never fails to plan the best things for us.

The train began moving, and I crouched down, and **in the name of Jesus commanded the disease to leave**. The old lady cried, "I'm healed. I know I'm healed." She stamped her leg and said, "I'm going to prove it." So when we stopped at another station, she marched up and down, and shouted, "I'm not going to the hospital." Once again our wonderful Jesus had proven Himself a Healer of the broken-hearted, a Deliverer of one that was bound.

Smith - "Wherever the Holy Ghost has the right of way, the gifts of the Spirit will be in manifestation; and where these gifts are never in manifestation, I question whether He is present."

#63   At one time I was so bound that no human power could help me. My wife was looking for me to pass away. There was no help. At that time I had just had a faint glimpse of Jesus as the Healer. For six months I had been suffering from appendicitis, occasionally getting temporary relief. I went to the mission of which I was a pastor, but I was brought to the floor in terrible and awful agony, and they brought me home to my bed. All night I was praying, pleading for deliverance, but none came. My wife was sure it was my home call and sent for a physician. He said that there was no possible chance for me, my body was too weak. Having had the appendicitis for six months, my whole system was drained, and, because of that, he thought that it was too late for an operation. He left my wife in a state of broken-heartedness.

After he had left, there came to our door a young man and an old lady. I knew that she was a woman of real prayer. They came upstairs to my room. This young man jumped on the bed and commanded the evil spirit to come out of me. He shouted, *"Come out, you devil; I command you to come out in the name of*

Jesus!" There was no chance for an argument, or for me to tell him that I would never believe that there was a devil inside of me. The thing had to go in the name of Jesus, and it went, and I was instantly healed.

I arose and dressed and went downstairs. I was still in the plumbing business, and I asked my wife, "Is there any work in? I am all right now, and I am going to work." I found there was a certain job to be done, and I picked up my tools and went off to do it. Just after I left, the doctor came in, put his hat down in the hall, and walked up to the bedroom. But the invalid was not there. "Where is Mr. Wigglesworth?" he asked. "Oh, doctor, he's gone out to work," said my wife. "You'll never see him alive again," said the doctor; "they'll bring him back a corpse."

Well, I'm the corpse. Since that time, in many parts of the world, the Lord has given me the privilege of praying for people with appendicitis; and I have seen a great many people up and dressed within a quarter of an hour from the time I prayed for them. We have a living Christ who is willing to meet people on every line.

Smith - People search everywhere today for things with which they can heal themselves & ignore the fact that the Balm of Gilead is within easy reach

#64   A number of years ago I met Brother D. W. Kerr and he gave me a letter of introduction to a brother in Zion City named Cook. I took his letter to Brother Cook, and he said, "God has sent you here." He gave me the addresses of six people and asked me to go and pray for them and meet him again at 12 o'clock. I got back at about 12:30 and he told me about a young man who was to be married the following Monday. His sweetheart was in Zion City dying of appendicitis. I went to the house and found that the physician had just been there and had pronounced that there was no hope. The mother was nearly out of her mind and was pulling her hair, and saying, "Is there no deliverance!" I said to her, "Woman, believe God and your daughter will be healed and be up and dressed in fifteen minutes." But the mother just went on screaming.

They took me into the bedroom, and I prayed for the girl and **Commanded the evil spirit to depart in the name of Jesus**. She cried, "I am healed." I said to her, "Do you want me to believe that you are healed? If you are healed, get up." She said, "You get out of the room, and I'll get up." In less than ten minutes the doctor came in. He wanted to know what had happened. She said, "A man came in and prayed for me, and I'm healed." The doctor pressed his finger right in the place that had been so sore, and the girl neither moaned nor cried. He said, **"This is God."** It made no difference whether he acknowledged it or not, I knew that God had worked. Our God is real in saving and healing power today. Our Jesus is just the same, yesterday, and today, and forever. He saves and heals today just as of old, and He wants to be your Savior and your Healer.

Smith - I don't often spend more than half an hour in prayer - but I never go more than half an hour without praying.

#72   I was called to a certain town in Norway. The hall seated approximately 1500 people. When I got to the place it was packed to the roof, and hundreds were trying to get in. There were some policemen there. The first thing I did was to preach to the people outside the building. Then I said to the policemen, "It hurts me very much that there are more people outside than inside, and I feel I must preach to the people. I would like you to get me the market place to preach in." They secured for me a great park and a big stand was erected, and I was able to preach to thousands. After the preaching, we had some amazing cases of healing.

One man came a hundred miles bringing his food with him. He had not been passing anything through his stomach for over a month as he had great cancer in his stomach. He was healed instantly at that meeting, and opening his parcel, he began eating before all the people. There was a young woman there with a stiff hand. Instead of the mother making the child use her arm she had allowed the child to keep the arm dormant until it was stiff, and she had grown up to be a young woman and was like the woman that was bowed down with the spirit of infirmity. As she stood before me, I cursed the spirit of infirmity in the name of Jesus. It was instantly cast out, and the arm was free. Then she waved it all over. At the close of the meeting the devil laid out two people with epileptic fits, **When the devil is manifesting himself, then is the time to deal with him.** Both of these people were wonderfully delivered, and they both stood up and thanked and praised the Lord. What a wonderful time we had.

Smith - "I want to help you decide that by the power of God, you will not be ordinary!"

#88   I received a telegram once urging me to visit a case about 200 miles from my home. As I went to this place, I met the father and mother and found them broken hearted. They lead me up a staircase to a room, and I saw a young woman on the floor, and five people were holding her down. She was a frail young woman, but the demonic power in her was greater than all those young men. As I went into the room, the evil powers looked out of her eyes, and they used her lips saying, "We are many, you can't cast us out." I said, "**Jesus can.**" He is more than enough in every situation. He is waiting for an opportunity to bless, heal and deliver. He is ready to save and to deliver souls. When we receive Jesus, it becomes a reality in us that, **"Greater is He that is in you**

than he that is in the world." He is greater than all the powers of darkness. No man can meet the devil in his own strength, but any man filled with the knowledge of Jesus, filled with His presence, filled with His power, filled with faith is more than a match for the powers of darkness. God has called us to be more than conquerors through Him that loved us.

The living Word is able to destroy satanic forces. There is power in the name of Jesus. I would that every window in the street had the name of Jesus written large upon it. **His name, through faith in His name.** Brought deliverance to this poor, bound soul. The dear woman was completely delivered, and they were able to give her back her child. That night there was heaven in that home and the father and mother, son and his wife were all united in glorifying Christ for His infinite grace. The next morning we had a gracious time in the breaking of bread. All things are wonderful with our wonderful Jesus. If you would dare rest your all upon Him, things would take place, and He would change your whole circumstance. In a moment, through the name of Jesus, a new life can be realized.

Smith - Lord, give us, Thy servants, great searching's of heart, great decisions of will and great assurances through the blood of Jesus.

Sermon: I Am the Lord That Healeth

#90   One day I had been visiting the sick, and was with a friend of mine, an architect when I saw a young man from his office coming down the road in a car, and holding in his hand a telegram. It contained a very urgent request that we go immediately to pray for a man who was dying. We went off in an auto as fast as possible and in about an hour and a half reached a large house in the country where the man who was dying resided.

Dr Michael H Yeager

There were two staircases in that house, and it was extremely convenient, for the doctors could go up and down one, and my friend and I could go up and down the other, and so we had no occasion to meet.

I found on arrival that had been physically hurt. The man's body had been broken; he was ruptured, and his bowels had been punctured in two places. The discharge from the bowels had formed abscesses, and blood poisoning had set in. The man's face had turned green. Two doctors were in attendance, but they saw that the case was beyond their power. They had telegraphed to London for a great specialist, and, when we arrived, they were at the railway station awaiting for this physician's arrival.

The man was very near death when we arrived and could not speak. I said to his wife, "If you desire, we will anoint and pray for him in the name of Jesus." She said, "That is why I sent for you." I anointed him in the name of the Lord and asked the Lord to raise him up. At that moment there was no change. (God often hides what He does. From day to day we find that God is doing wonderful things, and we receive reports of healings that have taken place that we heard nothing about at the time of our meetings. Only last night a woman came into the meeting suffering terribly. Her whole arm was filled with poison, and her blood was so poisoned that it was certain to bring her to her death. We rebuked the thing, and she was here this morning and told us that she was without pain and had slept all night, a thing she had not done for two months. To God be all the praise. You will find He will do this kind of thing all the time.)

As soon as we anointed and prayed for this brother, we went down the back staircase, and the three doctors came up the front staircase. As we arrived downstairs, I said to my friend who had come with me, "Friend let me have hold of your hands." We held each other's hands, and I said to him, "Look to God and let us agree together, according to Matthew 18:19, that this man shall be brought out of this death." We took the whole situation before God, and said, "Father, we believe."

Then the conflict began. The wife came down to us and said, "The doctors have got all their instruments out, and they are about to operate on him." I cried, "**What**? Look here; he's your husband, and I tell you this, if those men operate on him, he will die. Go back and tell them you cannot allow it." She went back to the doctors and said, "Give me ten minutes." They said, "We can't afford to; the man is dying, and it is your husband's only chance." She said, "I want ten minutes, and you don't touch him until I have those 10 minutes."

They went downstairs by one staircase, and we went up by the other. I said to the woman, "This man is your husband, and he cannot speak for himself. It is now the time for you to put your whole trust in God and prove Him wholly true. You can save him from a thousand doctors. You must stand with God and for God in this critical hour." After that, we came down, and the doctors went up. The wife faced those three doctors and said, "You will not touch my man's body. He is my husband. I am sure that if you operate on him, he will die, but he will live if you don't touch him."

Suddenly the man in the bed spoke. "God has done it," he said. They rolled back the bed clothes and the doctors examined him, and the abscesses were cut clear away. The nurse cleaned the place where they had been. The doctors could see the bowels still open, and they said to the wife, "We know that you have great faith, and we can see that a miracle has taken place. But you must let us unite these broken parts and put in silver tubes, and we know that your husband will be all right after that, and it need not interfere with your faith at all." She said to them, "God has done the first thing, and He can do the rest. No man shall touch him now." And God healed the whole thing. That same man is well and strong today. I can give his name and address to any who want it.

Smith - I do not ask my body how it feels. I TELL my body how it feels!

#91 My boys did not know anything else but to trust the Lord as the family Physician, and my youngest boy, George, cried out from the attic, "Dadda, come." I cried, "I cannot come. The whole thing is because of me. I shall have to repent and ask the Lord to forgive me." I made up my mind to humble myself before the whole church. Then I rushed to the attic and laid my hands on my boy in the **name of Jesus.** I placed my hands on his head, and the pain left and went lower down; he cried again, "Put your hands still lower." At last, the pain went right down to the feet and as I placed my hand on the feet be was completely delivered. Some evil power had evidently gotten a hold of him and as I laid my hands on the different parts of the body it left. (We have to see the difference between anointing the sick and **casting out demons.**) God will always be gracious when we humble ourselves before Him and come to a place of the brokenness of spirit.

Smith - No wavering! A definite faith brings a definite experience and a definite utterance.

#92 I was at a place one time ministering to a sick woman, and she said, "I'm very sick. I become all right for an hour, and then I have another attack." I saw that it was an **evil power** that was attacking her, and I learned something in that hour that I had never learned before. As **I moved my hand down her body in the name of the Lord that evil power seemed to move just ahead of my hands and as I moved them down further and further the evil power** went right out of her body and never returned.

CHAPTER THIRTEEN

CASTING OUT DEVILS - II

Smith - "The moment a man falls into sin, divine life ceases to flow, and his life becomes one of helplessness."

Sermon: On resurrection power

#99   Last week I went into a house where they were very much in great distress. A young woman was there who, they told me, had not been able to drink for six years. Her body had been rapidly degrading, but the Lord had inspired her with faith, and she said to her father, "O Father, I ought to have relief to-day. Somehow I feel this whole trouble ought to go to-day." I knew what it was. It was a **demon in the throat**. I believe that the devil is at the bottom of practically every evil in human lives. It was a serious thing to see that beautiful young woman, who, because of this one thing in her life, was so disorganized in her mind and body. I knew it was the power of Satan. How did I know? Because it attacked her at a vital point, and the thing had preyed on her mind, and she was filled with fear so that she said, "I dare not drink, for if I do I shall choke."

Deliverance to the captives. I asked the father and mother to go out of the room and then I said to the young woman, "You will be free and drink as much as you want when I have done with you if you will only believe. As sure as you are there you will drink as much as you want." I said further, "Our brethren are going out in the streets to preach to-night, and I shall be among them, and in our preaching, we will say definitely, 'Every one that will believe on the Lord Jesus Christ can be saved.' We will also tell them that everyone that believes can be healed. The Word of God shows us plainly that the Son of God bore our sins and our sicknesses at

Calvary. They will emphasize it over and over again. It is just as true to say, 'Himself took our infirmities and bare our sicknesses,' as it is to say, 'He was wounded for our transgressions, He was bruised for our iniquities.' " So I said to her, "Now do you believe?" She said, **"Yes, I believe that in the name of Jesus you can cast the evil power out."** I then laid my hands on her in the name of Jesus. "It is done, you drink."

She went out laughingly and drew the first glass of water and drank. She cried out, "Mother! Father! Brother! I have a drunk one glass!" There was joy in the house. What did it? It was the living faith of the Son of God. Oh, if we only knew how rich we are, and how near we are to the Fountain of life. "All things are possible to him that believeth."

From the sermon: The Discerning of Spirits

#115   I arrived one night at Gottenberg in Sweden and was asked to hold a meeting there. In the midst of the meeting, a man fell full length in the doorway. The evil spirit drew him down, manifesting itself and disturbing the whole meeting. I rushed to the door and laid hold of this man and cried out to the evil spirit within him, **"Come out, you devil! In the name of Jesus, we cast you out as an evil spirit."** I lifted him up and said, "Stand on your feet and walk in the name of Jesus." I don't know whether anybody in the meeting understood me except the interpreter, but the Devils knew what I said. I talked in English, but these devils in Sweden cleared out. A similar thing happened in Christiania.

Smith - It is impossible to overestimate the importance of being filled with the Spirit

#116   At one time there was brought to me a beautiful young woman who had been fascinated with some preacher, and just because he had not taken an interest in her on the line of courtship and marriage, the devil took advantage and made her fanatical and mad. They brought her 250 miles in that condition. She had previously received the Baptism in the Spirit. You ask, "can a demon come in to a person that has been baptized in the Holy Ghost?" Our only place of safety is if we are going on with God and in constantly being filled with the Holy Ghost. You must not forget Demas. He must have been baptized with the Holy Ghost for he appears to have been a right-hand worker with Paul, but the enemy got him to the place where he loved this present world, and he dropped off. When they brought this young woman to me, the evil power was immediately discerned and immediately **I cast this demonic thing out in the name of Jesus**. It was a great joy to present her before all the people in her right mind again. The devil has no power against the name of Jesus.

#118   I was at a meeting in Paisley in Scotland and came in touch with two young women. One of them wore a white blouse, but it was smeared with blood. They were in a great state of excitement. These two girls were telegraph operators and were precious young women, having received the Baptism in the Spirit. They were both longing to be missionaries. But whatever our spiritual state is we are subject to temptations. An evil power came to one of these young women and said, "If you obey me, I will make you one of the most wonderful missionaries that ever went out." This was just the devil or one of his agents acting as an angel of light. One of these young women was taken over immediately, and she became so fanatical that her sister saw there was something wrong and asked the overseer to allow them to have a little time off.

As she took her into a room, the power of Satan, endeavoring to imitate the Spirit of God, manifested itself in a voice and led this young woman to believe that the missionary enterprise would be unfolded that night if she would obey. This evil spirit said, "Don't tell anybody but your sister." I reckon that everything of God can be told, everybody. If you cannot preach what you live, your life is wrong. If you are afraid of telling what you do in secret, someday it will be told from the housetop. Don't think that it will be kept a secret. That which is pure cometh to the light. He that doeth truth cometh to the light that his deeds may be made manifest, that they are wrought in God.

The evil power went on to say to this girl, "You go to the railroad station tonight, and there will be a train coming in at 7:32. Buy a ticket for yourself and your sister. Then you will have six pence left. You will find a woman in a carriage dressed as a nurse, and opposite her will be a gentleman who has all the money you need." She bought her ticket and had just six pence left. The first thing came right. Next, the train came in at exactly 7:32. But the next thing did not come. They had run from the top to the bottom of that railroad train before it moved out and nothing turned out as they had been told. As soon as the train left the same voice came and said, "Over on the other platform." All that night until 9:30 p.m. these two young women were rushed from platform to platform.

As soon as it was 9:30 this same evil power said, "Now that I know you will obey me, I will make you the greatest missionaries that have ever lived." Always something big! They might have known it was all wrong. This evil power said, "This gentleman will take you to a certain bank at a certain corner in Glasgow where he will give all that money to you." Banks are not open at that time of night in Glasgow. If she had gone to the street this evil spirit mentioned, there probably would not have been a bank there. All they needed was a little common sense, and they would have seen that it was not the Lord. If you have your heart open for these kind of voices, you will soon get into a trap. We must ever remember that there are many evil spirits in the world.

Were these two people delivered? Yes, after terrible travail with God, they were perfectly delivered. Their eyes were opened to see that this thing was not of God but the devil. These two sisters are now laboring for the Lord in China and doing a blessed work for Him. If you do get into error on these lines, praise God there is a way out. I praise God that He will break us down till all pride leaves us. The worst pride we can have is the pride of exaltation of self.

Smith - As we think about that which is Holy, we become Holy. The more we think about Jesus, the more we become like Him.

#119   I knew some people who had a wonderful farm, very productive, in a very good neighborhood. They listened to voices telling them to sell everything and go to Africa. These voices so rushed them that they barely had time to sell out. They sold their property at a ridiculously low price. The same voices told them of a certain ship they were to sail on. When they got to the port, they found there wasn't a ship of that name. The difficulty was this trying to get them not to believe these false voices were not of God. They said perhaps it was the mind of the Lord to give them another ship, and the voice soon gave them the name of another ship.

When they reached Africa, they knew no language that was spoken there. But the voice drove them almost to total self-destruction. They had to come back, brokenhearted, shaken down to nothing, and having lost all confidence in everything. If only these people would have had enough sense to go to some men of God who were filled with the Spirit and seek their counsel, they would soon have been persuaded that these voices were not of God. But listening to these voices always brings about a spiritual pride that makes a man or woman think that they are superior to their brethren and that they are above taking counsel of men who they think are not so filled with the Spirit as they are. If you hear any voices that make you think that you are spiritually superior to those whom God has put in the church to rule the church, watch out that is surely the devil.

Sermon: The Power of Christ's Resurrection.

#123   One morning about eleven o'clock I saw a woman who was suffering from a tumor. She would be dead before the end of the day. A little blind girl led me to her bedside. Compassion overwhelmed me, and I wanted that woman to live for the child's sake. I said to the woman, "Do you want to live?" She could not speak. She just moved her finger. I anointed her with oil and said, "In the name of Jesus." There was a stillness of death that followed; and the pastor, looking at the woman, said to me, "She is gone."

When God pours in His compassion, it has resurrection power in it. I carried that woman across the room, put her against a wardrobe, and held her there. I said, **"In the name of Jesus, spirit of death, come out."** And soon her body began to tremble like a leaf. "In Jesus' name, walk," I said. I stepped away from her body. She did walk and went back to bed.

I told this story in the assembly. There was a doctor there, and he said, I am going to investigate this story." He went to the woman this happened to, and she told him it was perfectly true. She said, "I was in heaven, and I saw countless numbers all like Jesus. Then I heard a voice saying, 'Walk, in the name of Jesus.'"

There is power in the name of Jesus. Let us apprehend it, the power of His resurrection, the power of His compassion, the power of His love. Love will overcome the most difficult situations - there is nothing it cannot conquer.

Smith - "We must not be content with a mere theory of faith. We must have faith within us so that we move from the ordinary into the extraordinary."

#154   At Oakland a fine-looking young man, a slave to alcohol and nicotine, came along with his wife to see if I could heal him. They stated his case, and I **said: "Yes, I can heal you in Jesus Name."** I told him to put out his tongue, and **I cursed the demon power of alcohol and also cast out the demon power of nicotine.** The man knew that he was free. He afterwards became an earnest seeker and within 24 hours was baptized with the Holy Ghost. This is clearly confirming by the Scripture in **Mark 16:17 In My Name they shall cast out devils."**

Smith - Hear with the ear of faith! *See with the eye of Faith*

#177   I was prayed for in Melbourne, and **the evil spirit was commanded to come out.** I had a polypus growth in my nose. It had been there eighteen years. When I came home from Melbourne, the growth broke up and came away, for which I praise God. I had also it pain under my left breast which had troubled me twelve years. I think it was leakage of the heart, as sorrow had caused it in the first place. At times I used to vomit blood. I have deliverance from that also. All praise to our wonder-working Jesus!   MRS. T. SIMCOCK.

Smith - The Word of God is supernatural in origin, eternal in duration, infinite in scope, regenerative in power & infallible in authority.

#196 One night a woman came up the aisle, walking in pain, her body all doubled up, and she finally fell on the floor in front of the platform, the pain was so great that Brother Wigglesworth jumped off the platform and put his hands upon her, and said, **"In the name of Jesus I bind this pain and loose this woman."** Immediately she ran up and down the aisle, free from pain, and then went and sat down to listen to the message. She was perfectly whole. This demonstration had a great effect upon the crowd.

Smith - "It is impossible to overestimate the importance of being filled with the Spirit."

#206 Some nights the Evangelist had to pray for over five hundred people. Many of them coming hundreds of miles, bringing their sick with them – the blind, deaf, dumb, lame, paralyzed, consumptive, eaten up with cancer, tumor's, epilepsy, weak-minded, deranged, crippled, with rheumatism and many other kinds of diseases. They came to an increasing multitude, and God worked mighty miracles. Blind eyes being opened, deaf ears were unstopped, stammering tongues spoke plain, men on crutches put them over their shoulders and went away, stiff joints were made supple, headaches and fevers vanished, **asthma was cursed as an evil power and cast out in the Name of Jesus**. It was a wonderful sight to see them coming, and to know that those who had faith, went away rejoicing, in a Living, Loving, Tender-hearted Savior, who had delivered them from the power of the devil that had bound them for weeks and months, and years, or a lifetime.

We know that many wonderful cures have been wrought in this way, eruptions have vanished, and a case of insanity was wonderfully helped. The father brought a handkerchief for his son in the asylum; after it had been prayed over it was taken to the asylum, placed on the son's head, and he at once began to speak like a normal being. Another one was taken to a sanatorium, and placed on a consumptive boy; the message brought from the sanatorium says the boy is wonderfully better, putting on flesh and looking healthy. Drunkard's lives have been changed by these means, desires for gambling have gone, and many wonderful deliverances have taken place. Glory to Jesus.

You Cannot Cast out the Flesh

I have run into many people through the years who wanted me to cast devils out of them, who did not have devils. I am not saying that there was not any satanic activity, but they were not demon possessed. They might have been Obsessed, Depressed, Oppressed, but they were not Possessed! I have seen people obsessed with the thought that they were Possessed! The fact of the matter is they did not need to have devils cast out of them, but they needed to cast down thoughts and imaginations.

2 Corinthians 10:4 (For the weapons of our warfare are not carnal, but mighty through God to the pulling down of strong holds;)5 Casting down imaginations, and every high thing that exalteth itself against the knowledge of God, and bringing into captivity every thought to the obedience of Christ;

Proverbs 15:26 The thoughts of the wicked are an abomination to the Lord: but the words of the pure are pleasant words.

Isaiah 55:7 Let the wicked forsake his way, and the unrighteous man his thoughts: and let him return unto the Lord, and he will have mercy upon him; and to our God, for he will abundantly pardon.

Proverbs 23:7 For as he thinketh in his heart, so is he: Eat and drink, saith he to thee; but his heart is not with thee.

Philippians 4:7 And the peace of God, which passeth all understanding, shall keep your hearts and minds through Christ Jesus.8 Finally, brethren, whatsoever things are true, whatsoever things are honest, whatsoever things are just, whatsoever things are pure, whatsoever things are lovely, whatsoever things are of good report; if there be any virtue, and if there be any praise, think on these things.9 Those things, which ye have both learned, and received, and heard, and seen in me, do: and the God of peace shall be with you.

You Have To Crucify the Flesh

People will not like to hear this, but there is a lot of spiritual laziness that is going on in the body of Christ. People do not want to take the time to renew their minds. People do not want to turn off the perversion that is coming through secular entertainment and vain amusements. When we are not following after Christ but are giving ourselves to the world, the enemy finds a wide open door to come in and harass us. So many people in the body of Christ are tormented because they are out of the will of God. The enemy has blinded their eyes to the cause of their torments. When you are tormented, you cannot help but torment others.

Romans 12:1 I beseech you therefore, brethren, by the mercies of God, that ye present your bodies a living sacrifice, holy, acceptable unto God, which is your reasonable service.2 And be not conformed to this world: but be ye transformed by the renewing of your mind, that ye may prove what is that good, and acceptable, and perfect, will of God.

There are many Scriptures that tell us to mortify, crucify, and bring into subjection our mortal flesh!

Galatians 2:20 I am crucified with Christ: nevertheless I live; yet not I, but Christ liveth in me: and the life which I now live in the flesh I live by the faith of the Son of God, who loved me, and gave himself for me.

Galatians 5:24 And they that are Christ's have crucified the flesh with the affections and lusts.

Galatians 6:14 But God forbid that I should glory, save in the cross of our Lord Jesus Christ, by whom the world is crucified unto me, and I unto the world.

Romans 6:13 Neither yield ye your members as instruments of unrighteousness unto sin: but yield yourselves unto God, as those that are alive from the dead, and your members as instruments of righteousness unto God.

Romans 8:13 For if ye live after the flesh, ye shall die: but if ye through the Spirit do mortify the deeds of the body, ye shall live.

Colossians 3:5 Mortify therefore your members which are upon the earth; fornication, uncleanness, inordinate affection, evil concupiscence, and covetousness, which is idolatry:6 For which things' sake the wrath of God cometh on the children of disobedience:

1 Corinthians 15:31 I protest by your rejoicing which I have in Christ Jesus our Lord, I die daily.

1 Peter 2:11 Dearly beloved, I beseech you as strangers and pilgrims, abstain from fleshly lusts, which war against the soul;

1 Corinthians 6:9 Know ye not that the unrighteous shall not inherit the kingdom of God? Be not deceived: neither fornicators, nor idolaters, nor adulterers, nor effeminate, nor abusers of themselves with mankind,10 Nor thieves, nor covetous, nor drunkards, nor revilers, nor extortioners, shall inherit the kingdom of God.

Terrible Things Happen When You Listen to the Devil!

*31. My Dad Died trying to get Away from it all!

Ninety percent of the time when I give a prophetic word to someone in the spirit, I do not remember what I said. Sometimes I'm just so lost in the Holy Ghost; it is like I've entered into another world. God by his Spirit, speaking through people will bring wonderful deliverance and healing to their lives. Now when someone is talking about moving up into the mountains, living in a cabin, and getting away from everybody on a permanent bases, you know that they are in the flesh. Jesus did not want us to be taken out of the world, but to be kept in the midst of it. God wants us to be witnesses, salt and light, ambassadors for the King of Kings and Lord of Lords.

My earthly father thought it was the ultimate dream to live in a cabin away from everybody else. He wanted to be all alone, so he left my mother, breaking her heart, and then he completely closed the door on all of his children except for one that is my younger brother. Yes, he ended up living in a cabin all alone, but unbeknownst to him, birds had built a nest in the chimney. There was enough airflow to keep the smoke out of the cabin room, yet not the carbon monoxide. He was 68 years old and in good health, but the carbon monoxide poisoning still got him. He allowed this satanic thought to take a hold of his mind that he didn't need anybody but this cabin. This desire to be all alone might have seemed wonderful to him, and yet is what the devil used to kill him. The enemy uses a lot of silly ideas to kill people.

*32.The devil was in the Details!
(2010)

In the early spring of 2010, my wife and I had rented a hotel room at Bethany Beach Delaware. We were there to get away from everything to finish the book I was writing. The name of this book was "The Horrors of Hell, Splendors of Heaven". In the early spring, you can rent a hotel room very cheap at the beach because the tourist season had not yet started. The beach is deserted because it is still too cold to enjoy the waters, so it is a wonderful time just to walk the miles and miles of shore talking to the Lord.

As we were there, I received a phone call from a wife of one of the elders in the church we had in Maryland. In 1996 I had started this church under the direct leading of the Holy Ghost. After I had pastored this church for approximately five years, I installed a full-time pastor. After I installed this pastor, another gentleman who had been in our church ministering, became close to this pastor. This particular brother immediately tried to strip this church out from under my authority. I am not a man who is enthusiastic with authority but simply knowing I have responsibility. Actually one of my flaws is that I do not take the authority that God has given to me fully, to protect God's people.

By the grace of God I was able to prevent this from happening, but in the process, the name of the place was changed to another name. I only remained on the board as a deterrent from any major change taking place in this congregation. In the event of the joining of this church with another church, or the instalment of a new pastor, or the closing down or selling of the church property according to the bylaws and Constitution, I must be involved and in agreement.

As my wife and I were in Delaware, I received a phone call from one of the sisters who had been on the board almost from the beginning of the church. She informed me with great distress that the pastor was about to merge the church with another church not of like persuasion, turning over all the authority to this new pastor/so-called apostle. I informed her that he could not legally do this. They would have to call an official meeting, and I would have to be present. If the present pastor endeavored to pass off this church to another church, I would take them to court. Oh, but brother Mike don't you know we are not to take a brother to court. I was not suing anybody, just simply making sure they abided by the governing laws that were established for that congregation.

Acts 25:10-11, Then said Paul, I stand at Caesar's judgment seat, where I ought to be judged: to the Jews have I done no wrong, as thou very well knowest. For if I be an offender, or have committed any thing worthy of death, I refuse not to die: but if there be none of these things whereof these accuse me, no man may deliver me unto them. I appeal unto Caesar.

This precious sister informed the leadership of the church of my statement. When my wife and I finally came back to Pennsylvania, a meeting was set up for us to get together with everybody involved at their main facility. The day came for the meeting. My wife and I arrived early, and as we stepped onto the property, it was obvious that those who had been conniving were very upset. We did not go into this meeting acting arrogant or pushing our way around. As the meeting was called to order, I simply listened to what they had to say. Throughout this meeting, I continued to pray. As I looked around, I saw an African-American brother who was probably in his early 40s. The spirit of the Lord told me that this brother was called to be the next new pastor. I do not think at the time I realized that he was the assistant pastor, but that he had been kept out of the loop by the present head pastor.

Finally, my time came to speak in the meeting. I informed them of the Constitution and the bylaws that this church was obligated to remain in the spiritual persuasion for which it was started. The congregation which had been invited, and who had been attending the church services, was not of the same spiritual persuasion. Therefore this merger would not happen.

After the meeting, my wife and I were sitting in our car when the head pastor came storming up to our vehicle. My window was down as he began to castigate, yell and act very strange towards my wife and me. I spoke to him very softly, never raising my voice once. I tried to speak divine wisdom into his life. I will not repeat any of the words that were spoken that night from this brother, but they were not of God. Eventually, he ran out of steam, broke down crying and was almost beside himself. My wife and I spoke to him very softly, encouraging him to seek God.

I wrapped my arms around him as he was up against the vehicle, asking God to help him. He had poured himself into this church for over a decade. He was the one who had believed for the facility they were now in. After we were done speaking to him, it was like he was completely deflated. He spun around and walked away, never having spoken to us again. As he left, I knew in my heart what was going on by the spirit of God. The Lord spoke to me and said he was involved in a certain sin. I told my wife what the spirit of the Lord had spoken to me. She informed me that the Lord had spoken to her the same thing. I am not being judgmental of this brother because it is so easy for the devil to set us up.

After that meeting, it was obvious to everybody that this merger was not going to happen. The church that had been given all kinds of promises by the pastor. In a very short time, it was revealed that indeed he had been involved in sin. The next thing we knew him and his wife were separated. He resigned from the church, leaving everything in the hands of the board. To this day, I still pray and stand in the gap, hoping he will be restored to Christ.

We installed the assistant pastor, whom the Lord spoke to my heart would become the head pastor. He has been doing a wonderful job at his new assignment. Yes, he has had many challenges, but God is blessing him and the congregation in a wonderful way. If we would not have stood our grounds, I am convinced this church would have been brought to complete and utter devastation. This church is still a wonderful light in their community where they are ministering to the needy and the hurting.

*33. Like a moth to the flame

Jesus said, "The Prince of this world comes, and he can find nothing in me." I'm sorry to say that this is not the experience of any Christian in this world. There are many things within our hearts, emotions, and minds that are so deeply buried that we do not even realize that they are there until we are put through the flames of trials and temptation. The enemy of our soul is constantly trying to find ways to destroy us, always probing our defenses. There is a doctrine out there that declares that once one is born again, the carnal nature with its lusts and sinful desires is dead. Oh, how I wish that this were true because that would make life so easy! However, scripture declares otherwise as well as my personal experience in my Christian walk. Evil desires often just lie there dormant, like a seed in the soil, waiting to spring forth. The Bible school that I went to taught that philosophy. I believe that the results would be shocking if one would follow up on the lives of the various graduates from this faith-based Bible school. Many of them have returned to the ways of the world since they lacked a solid foundation in the entire Word of God.

Too often, Christians chase one tangent after another, failing to digest the entire Word of God. Their diets are limited, and they become spiritually malnourished, never achieving maturity in the things of God. Even when I was at this world-famous faith school, the founder of this movement stood up with tears in his eyes talking about the blatant sin that was going on among the students.

Okay, back to my embarrassing story that I do not want to share with you, but maybe it could help to rescue your life. Before I had met my wife, I had been dating my childhood sweetheart who was my next-door neighbor. I'm ashamed to say that I had a relationship with her sexually before I knew Christ. Mentally and emotionally, she had captured my heart at a time when neither of us were born again. Actually, I discovered years later that she had not been faithful while I was in the Navy, but that is neither here nor there. We had planned on getting married once I finished my tour in the Navy but three months before the end of my military enlistment, I had a supernatural encounter with Jesus Christ.

I was gloriously born again and delivered from all of my disgustingly wicked habits and corrupt lifestyle. I enthusiastically wrote my wife to be what God had gloriously done for me. It wasn't long before I received her response: a dear John letter telling me to hit the road, Jack, and don't look back. She wanted nothing to do with my me or my relationship with Christ. That was the best thing that could have happened to me because it liberated me to go all the way for God. Unbeknownst to me, I never did fully let her go in my heart.

Over 20 years had passed with me being married to my precious wife Kathleen, the mother of our five children. We were going through a rather rough time in our lives; hence, my thoughts began to stray back to my "first love". I never spoke of my past transgressions with any glee or excitement in front of my children or my wife. I knew that could be used against them. So, if I ever shared with them what I had been through, including the fact that I had known a woman before I knew their mother, it was always with tears in my eyes. This is a major tool the devil can use against our children. Be very careful when you talk about the good old times because, as you very well know, they probably really weren't such great times after all.

Despite this, I began to wonder what ever happened to my old girlfriend. I did a little bit of investigation and discovered that she had been divorced and was now single. I should have immediately taken authority and cast down those thoughts, but our hearts are so easily led astray. I began to think about her more and more frequently. Suddenly, an idea came into my stupid, silly head which I should've known was of the devil, but I was deceived. I thought about going back to my hometown and looking her up. Of course, during this time, there was no internet that would give me access to this information. I knew in my heart that I should not be thinking like this but, hey, it was just an innocent thought. I was not planning on anything that would be wrong anyway, I just simply wanted to see how she was going and to talk about the old times.

What a lie from the pit of hell! The Scriptures clearly tell us that we are extremely weak and easily led astray. This is why the minute an evil thought arises, we must immediately submit to the Lordship of Jesus Christ, resist the devil and he will flee from us. But this was not my case. I got it into my stupid head that I was going to go back to Hometown, Wisconsin and look up my old girlfriend. I went to my wife telling her that I was missing my family back home and that I would like to take a ride out there to reach out to some of my old friends and immediate family. She did not think for a moment that something else was going on in my heart. This is exactly how the devil sets us up. I was a little bit surprised with her response because she actually thought that it was a good idea.

Now that the idea had really taken root in my mind, I began to make plans. There was only one problem; I didn't know where she was now living, and the only one who could tell me was her immediate family. At one time, her older brother was my best friend, but he had completely rejected me since I had given my heart to Jesus and became a minister of the gospel.

I decided that before I went out to Wisconsin, I needed to find out where she was. I certainly didn't want to go on a wild goose chase. Believe me, at the time I had no intentions of doing anything evil, but I was like a moth that had been led to the flame. I had kept her older brother's telephone number with me through the years because they had a tool and die shop in East Troy, Wisconsin. I finally decided to make the move, calling the telephone number to their business. Her older brother answered the phone. I spoke up that it was me, his old buddy. I carried on a conversation with him for a while, catching up on the lives of past acquaintances in the area, asking how they were all doing. I was trying maneuver the conversation to spring my question in a very crafty, sly and subtle way. I finally got around to it and came right out and asked him, Hey, Mike, how is your younger sister doing, naming her by name, and asking where she now lived?

His response really surprised me because out of his mouth came nothing but cuss words, telling me in no uncertain terms that what his sister was doing, where she was at, and what was happening in her life was none of my blankety-blank business. Wow, he really laid it on me, but I can truly say —**THANK GOD HE DID!**

He knew I was married, pastoring a church and had children. This man did not know God and did not want to know God, but when I asked about his sister, such indignation rose up inside of him that he literally would've torn my head off if I would have been in the same room with him. Now, this may not sound like it was God but it was God using him to rescue my poor bacon out of the fire.

After his rant, the lights came flooding into my mind and my heart and at that very moment, **I saw that the devil had set me up**. There is zero doubt that if I would had gone to Wisconsin; I would have been devoured spiritually. I would've lost my precious wife, my children, my ministry and possibly even my salvation. I was like a moth being drawn to the fire, in which case I would have been consumed like so many others who have allowed the devil to lead them astray on the path to destruction. Thank you, Lord Jesus, for humbling me knowing that even a notorious sinner was more in tune with Truth than I was!

1 Corinthians 10:12 Wherefore let him that thinketh he standeth take heed lest he fall.

2 Corinthians 11:3 But I fear, lest by any means, as the serpent beguiled Eve through his subtilty, so your minds should be corrupted from the simplicity that is in Christ.

*34. Fox in the Hen House (1998)

Strange things seemed to be happening at the church. I would walk into the office, and everybody would suddenly hush up. I found out later that there were those who were spreading horrendous gossip about my family and me. Most people when they hear gossip, instead of going to the person being gossiped about, swallow it hook, line and sinker. My poor hiring decisions began to unravel. The church had entered a time of rapid growth and, instead of waiting on God to make sure that I had hired the right people, I was motivated out of my desperate need for help. The harvest truly is great, and the laborers are few. I truly believe that there are many people in the so-called ministry today, not because of their love for Christ, but for self-glorification and financial gain. In retelling these stories, I try to use wisdom because I am not trying to slander people or to misrepresent the situations that I found myself in. In no way am I claiming that I was the perfect pastor or did everything just right.

I had three groups of leadership in our church. There were the elders, who were all solid men in the Word. They stuck with me through thick and thin. And then I had the deacons which served as directors over departments. Rounding it all out was the pastoral staff.

Then, along came another man that my wife knew. She had gone to school with his wife. My wife told me not to hire him! But, since he was so good with people and was such a natural salesman, where I was kind of rough and blunt, I rationalized my decision. Because I have an apostolic call on my life, many people have misunderstood me. Through the year's people, have told me that I was not a pastor. They could not recognize nor spiritually discern the difference between a pastor and an apostle. I used this as my excuse to hire him; to have him fill in the gaps of my short-comings. I complained, "Lord, you know that I'm not really a pastor, I am apostolic, and people just do not comprehend the difference." My whining swung the doors wide open, allowing the enemy to really begin to work, especially when I hired an administrator that I should never have hired.

This person first approached me as a volunteer. Over time, I began to let this person make more and more decisions, convinced that a laborer was worthy of his hire. I gave into this trickery. I do not hold these people responsible since I was the one in charge. (The buck stops here!)

Eventually, I heard that the brother who my wife told me (in no uncertain terms) not to hire as an assistant pastor was meeting privately with my deacons and was stirring the pot. I had hired him in part because of his social charm, but that was now coming back and kicking me in the head. He was going to the deacon's homes and spending personal time with each one of them. A warning began to buzz in my head. I confronted him, notifying him of his inappropriate conduct and informing him that he needed to stop. But, of course, he did not. After he had left, I discovered that he had been spreading all kinds of fabrications about me. One such example is that when he would visit the sick per my request; when he did if he did, he would tell them that I commanded him not to visit them. Instead, he would tell them, "I came to see you anyway because of the great love that I have for you." Often, we have an Absalom in our midst, and we are completely clueless about it.

Before I knew what was happening, there was a full-fledged rebellion going on in the church. My world began to fall apart. The elders I had with me at the time stood faithful and strong. (Of course, I'm only sharing with you the tip of the iceberg.) The seven deacons had given themselves over to a wrong spirit. Those we follow will direct our course. We had better be very cautious who we choose to follow. Of course, I hold myself accountable for my own poor decisions.

I was being deceived, which allowed a spirit of deception to hover over our church. This so-called brother tried to take over the church. Praise God; the Lord Himself interceded, and the man failed. He took the deacons, their wives and other members of the congregation and went down the road about 18 miles where they started a new church that did not last very long. Most of the people who followed this particular man ended up experiencing tragic circumstances. My heart still reaches out to them. I pray for complete restoration and healing! This so-called brother is still in prison at the writing of this book. He never did come back and repent. But, of course, that's between him and God. Just keep your hearts sweet, loving and forgiving even as Christ forgave us.

CHAPTER FOURTEEN

22 Major Weapons of the Devil!

1) Deception, a lie, wiles

Matthew 24:4 And Jesus answered and said unto them, Take heed that no man deceive you. **Matthew 24:5** For many shall come in my name, saying, I am Christ; and shall deceive many. **Galatians 6:7** Be not deceived; God is not mocked: for whatsoever a man soweth, that shall he also reap. **Ephesians 5:6** Let no man deceive you with vain words: for because of these things cometh the wrath of God upon the children of disobedience. **James 1:22** But be ye doers of the word, and not hearers only, deceiving your own selves. **John 8:44** Ye are of your father the devil, and the lusts of your father ye will do. He was a murderer from the beginning, and abode not in the truth, because there is no truth in him. When he speaketh a lie, he speaketh of his own: for he is a liar, and the father of it.

2) Cares of this World -

Matthew 13:22 He also that received seed among the thorns is he that heareth the word; and the care of this world, and the deceitfulness of riches, choke the word, and he becometh unfruitful. **Mark 4:19** And the cares of this world, and the deceitfulness of riches, and the lusts of other things entering in, choke the word, and it becometh unfruitful. Philippians 4:6 Be careful for nothing; but in everything by prayer and supplication with thanksgiving let your requests be made known unto God.1 **Peter 5:7** Casting all your care upon him; for he careth for you. **Matthew 6:25** Therefore I say unto you, Take no thought for your life, what ye shall eat, or what ye shall drink; nor yet for your body, what ye shall put on. Is not the life more than meat, and the body than raiment?

3) Covetousness

Luke 12:15 And he said unto them, Take heed, and beware of covetousness: for a man's life consisteth not in the abundance of the things which he possesseth. **Luke 16:13** No servant can serve two masters: for either he will hate the one, and love the other; or else he will hold to the one, and despise the other. Ye cannot serve God and mammon.**14** And the Pharisees also, who were covetous, heard all these things: and they derided him.**1 Timothy 6:9** But they that will be rich fall into temptation and a snare, and into many foolish and hurtful lusts, which drown men in destruction and perdition.**10** For the love of money is the root of all evil: which while some coveted after, they have erred from the faith, and pierced themselves through with many sorrows.**11** But thou, O man of God, flee these things; and follow after righteousness, godliness, faith, love, patience, meekness.

4) Lust - flesh, eyes,

1 John 2:15 Love not the world, neither the things that are in the world. If any man love the world, the love of the Father is not in him.**16** For all that is in the world, the lust of the flesh, and the lust of the eyes, and the pride of life, is not of the Father, but is of the world.**17** And the world passeth away, and the lust thereof: but he that doeth the will of God abideth forever. **James 1:13** Let no man say when he is tempted, I am tempted of God: for God cannot be tempted with evil, neither tempteth he any man:**14** But every man is tempted, when he is drawn away of his own lust, and enticed.**15** Then when lust hath conceived, it bringeth forth sin: and sin, when it is finished, bringeth forth death. **[40 times it talks about lust in the New Testament]**

5)Pride –

 Proverbs 8:13 The fear of the Lord is to hate evil: pride, and arrogancy, and the evil way, and the froward mouth, do I hate. **Proverbs 16:18** Pride goeth before destruction, and an haughty spirit before a fall. **Proverbs 29:23** A man's pride shall bring him low: but honour shall uphold the humble in spirit. **James 4:6** But he giveth more grace. Wherefore he saith, God resisteth the proud, but giveth grace unto the humble.**1 Peter 5:5** Likewise, ye younger, submit yourselves unto the elder. Yea, all of you be subject one to another, and be clothed with humility: for God resisteth the proud, and giveth grace to the humble.

6) Ignorance

Hosea 4:6 My people are destroyed for lack of knowledge: because thou hast rejected knowledge, I will also reject thee, that thou shalt be no priest to me:-----**Isaiah 5:13** Therefore my people are gone into captivity, because they have no knowledge: and their honourable men are famished, and their multitude dried up with thirst. **Job 42:5** I have heard of thee by the hearing of the ear: but now mine eye seeth thee.**6** Wherefore I abhor myself, and repent in dust and ashes.

7) Imitation - FALSE

Proverbs 11:1 A false balance is abomination to the Lord: but a just weight is his delight. **Proverbs 25:14** Whoso boasteth himself of a false gift is like clouds and wind without rain. **Jeremiah 5:31** The prophets prophesy falsely, and the priests bear rule by their means; and my people love to have it so: and what will ye do in the end thereof? [false Gospel, angel of light, another Jesus]**Mark 13:22** For false Christs and false prophets shall rise, and shall shew signs and wonders, to seduce, if it were possible, even the elect.

8) Temptation

Matthew 4:3 And when the tempter came to him, he said, If thou be the Son of God, command that these stones be made bread. **Matthew 6:13** And lead us not into temptation, but deliver us from evil: For thine is the kingdom, and the power, and the glory, forever. Amen. **Hebrews 2:18** For in that he himself hath suffered being tempted, he is able to succour them that are tempted.

9) Frustration,

implies making vain or ineffectual all efforts however vigorous or persistent/ **Galatians 2:21** I do not frustrate the grace of God: for if righteousness come by the law, then Christ is dead in vain.

10) Hate =

bitterness, resentment, anger, unforgiveness, **Hebrews 12:14** Follow peace with all men, and holiness, without which no man shall see the Lord:**15** Looking diligently lest any man fail of the grace of God; lest any root of bitterness springing up trouble you, and thereby many be defiled; **Ephesians 4:31** Let all bitterness, and wrath, and anger, and clamour, and evil speaking, be put away from you, with all malice: **Matthew 6:15** But if ye forgive not men their trespasses, neither will your Father forgive your trespasses.

11) Fear –

intimidation, panic, *be careful for nothing......Tells us not to FEAR = 365 times in bible!**2 Timothy 1:7** For God hath not given us the spirit of fear; but of power, and of love, and of a sound mind. **Joshua 8:1** And the Lord said unto Joshua, Fear not, neither be thou dismayed: Joshua 1:9 Have not I commanded thee? Be strong and of a good courage; be not afraid, neither be thou dismayed: for the Lord thy God is with thee whithersoever thou goest. **Isaiah 41:10** Fear thou not; for I am with thee: be not dismayed; for I am thy God: I will strengthen thee; yea, I will help thee; yea, I will uphold thee with the right hand of my righteousness.

12) Persecution –

Matthew 5:10 Blessed are they which are persecuted for righteousness' sake: for theirs is the kingdom of heaven. Romans 8:35 Who shall separate us from the love of Christ? shall tribulation, or distress, or persecution, or famine, or nakedness, or peril, or sword? Romans 12:14 Bless them which persecute you: bless, and curse not.2 Timothy 3:12 Yea, and all that will live godly in Christ Jesus shall suffer persecution.

13) Affliction =

sickness, disease, mental and emotional, Psalm 34:19 Many are the afflictions of the righteous: but the Lord delivereth him out of them all.2 Corinthians 4:17 For our light affliction, which is but for a moment, worketh for us a far more exceeding and eternal weight of glory;2 Timothy 4:5 But watch thou in all things, endure afflictions, do the work of an evangelist, make full proof of thy ministry.

14) Confusion =

Job 10:15 If I be wicked, woe unto me; and if I be righteous, yet will I not lift up my head. I am full of confusion; therefore see thou mine affliction; Psalm 71:1 In thee, O Lord, do I put my trust: let me never be put to confusion.1 Corinthians 14:33 For God is not the author of confusion, but of peace, as in all churches of the saints. James 3:16 For where envying and strife is, there is confusion and every evil work.[JOB COMPLETELY CONFUSED]

15) Oppression –

Job 35:9 By reason of the multitude of oppressions they make the oppressed to cry: they cry out by reason of the arm of the mighty. Acts 10:38 How God anointed Jesus of Nazareth with the Holy Ghost and with power: who went about doing good, and healing all that were oppressed of the devil; for God was with him.

16) Depression –

Psalm 143:7-8 [Full Chapter] Hear me speedily, O Lord: my spirit faileth: hide not thy face from me, lest I be like unto them that go down into the pit. Cause me to hear thy lovingkindness in the morning; for in thee do I trust: cause me to know the way wherein I should walk; for I lift up my soul unto thee. **Numbers 21:4** And they journeyed from mount Hor by the way of the Red sea, to compass the land of Edom: and the soul of the people was much discouraged because of the way. **Colossians 3:21** Fathers, provoke not your children to anger, lest they be discouraged.**1 Kings :4** But he himself went a day's journey into the wilderness, and came and sat down under a juniper tree: and he requested for himself that he might die; and said, It is enough; now, O Lord, take away my life; for I am not better than my fathers.

17) Obsession, addictions –

1 Kings 11:1 But king Solomon loved many strange women, together with the daughter of Pharaoh, women of the Moabites, Ammonites, Edomites, Zidonians, and Hittites:

18) Possession –

Matthew 4:24 And his fame went throughout all Syria: and they brought unto him all sick people that were taken with divers diseases and torments, and those which were possessed with devils, and those which were lunatic, and those that had the palsy; and he healed them. **Matthew 8:16** When the even was come, they brought unto him many that were possessed with devils: and he cast out the spirits with his word, and healed all that were sick: **Matthew 8:28** And when he was come to the other side into the country of the Gergesenes, there met him two possessed with devils, coming out of the tombs, exceeding fierce, so that no man might pass by that way. **Matthew 8:33** And they that kept them fled, and went their ways into the city, and told everything, and what was befallen to the possessed of the devils. **Matthew 9:32** As they went out, behold, they brought to him a dumb man possessed with a devil. **Matthew 12:22** Then was brought unto him one possessed with a devil, blind, and dumb: and he healed him, insomuch that the blind and dumb both spake and saw.

19) Idolatry –

1 Corinthians 10:14 Wherefore, my dearly beloved, flee from idolatry. **Galatians 5:20** Idolatry, witchcraft, hatred, variance, emulations, wrath, strife, seditions, heresies, **Colossians 3:5** Mortify therefore your members which are upon the earth; fornication, uncleanness, inordinate affection, evil concupiscence, and covetousness, which is idolatry:

20) Laziness –

Revelation 3:16 So then because thou art lukewarm, and neither cold nor hot, I will spue thee out of my mouth. **Proverbs 21:25** The desire of the slothful killeth him; for his hands refuse to labour. **Proverbs 22:13** The slothful man saith, There is a lion without, I shall be slain in the streets.**2 Thessalonians 3:10** For even when we were with you, this we commanded you, that if any would not work, neither should he eat.

21) Self-Centeredness =

me-ism, I, I, I,- sefish, **1 Corinthians 10:24** Let no one seek his own good, but the good of his neighbor. **Philippians 2:4** - Look not every man on his own things, but every man also on the things of others.**2 Timothy 3:2-4** - For men shall be lovers of their own selves, covetous, boasters, proud, blasphemers, disobedient to parents, unthankful, unholy, **Philippians 2:3-4** - [Let] nothing [be done] through strife or vainglory; but in lowliness of mind let each esteem other better than themselves.

22) Complainers,

fault finders, unthankful, whiners and grippers, = **Jude 1:16** These are murmurers, complainers, walking after their own lusts; and their mouth speaketh great swelling words, having men's persons in admiration because of advantage. **Numbers 14:27** How long shall I bear with this evil congregation, which murmur against me? I have heard the murmurings of the children of Israel, which they murmur against me. **Ephesians 4:29** Let no corrupt communication proceed out of your mouth, but that which is good to the use of edifying, that it may minister grace unto the hearers.

Books Written by Doc Yeager:

"Living in the Realm of the Miraculous #1."
"I need God Cause I'm Stupid."
"The Miracles of Smith Wigglesworth"
"How Faith Comes 28 WAYS"
"Horrors of Hell, Splendors of Heaven"
"The Coming Great Awakening"
"Sinners in The Hands of an Angry GOD,"
"Brain Parasite Epidemic"
"My JOURNEY to HELL" - illustrated for teenagers
"Divine Revelation of Jesus Christ"
"My Daily Meditations"
"Holy Bible of JESUS CHRIST"
"War In The Heavenlies - (Chronicles of Micah)"
"Living in the Realm of the Miraculous #2."
"My Legal Rights to Witness"
"Why We (MUST) Gather! - 30 Biblical Reasons"
"My Incredible, Supernatural, Divine Experiences"
"Living in the Realm of the Miraculous #3."
"How GOD Leads & Guides! - 20 Ways"
"Weapons of Our Warfare"
"How You Can Be Healed"
"Hell Is For Real"
"Heaven Is For Real"
"God Still Heals"
"God Still Provides"
"God Still Protects"
"God Still Gives Dreams & Visions."
"God Still Does Miracles"
"God Still Gives Prophetic Words"
"God Still Confirms His Word With Power"
"Life Changing Quotes of Smith Wigglesworth"

Dr Michael H Yeager

ABOUT THE AUTHOR

Dr. Michael and Kathleen Yeager have served as pastors/apostles, missionaries, evangelists, broadcasters, and authors for over four decades. They flow in the gifts of the Holy Spirit, teaching the Word of God with wonderful signs and miracles following in confirmation of God's Word. In 1983, they began Jesus is Lord Ministries International, Biglerville, PA 17307.

Websites Connected to Doc Yeager

www.docyeager.com

www.jilmi.org

www.wbntv.org

Dr Michael H Yeager

Made in the USA
Coppell, TX
20 June 2020